Atlantic Canada
Quiz

How much do you know about Atlantic Canada?

Calvin Coish

NIMBUS
PUBLISHING

Nimbus Publishing Limited
PO Box 9166
Halifax, NS B3K 5M8
(902) 455-4286
www.nimbus.ca

Printed and bound in Canada

Library and Archives Canada Cataloguing in Publication

Coish, E. Calvin, 1948-
Atlantic Canada quiz : how much do you know about
Atlantic Canada? / Calvin Coish.

ISBN 978-1-55109-647-6

1. Atlantic Provinces—Miscellanea. I. Title.

FC2005.C64 2008   971.5   C2008-901459-6

We acknowledge the financial support of the Government of Canada through the Book Publishing Industry Development Program (BPIDP) and the Canada Council, and of the Province of Nova Scotia through the Department of Tourism, Culture and Heritage for our publishing activities.

QUIZ #1

1. In Newfoundland, what is a growler?
2. *King's Bounty*, by this Nova Scotia author, was published in 1978.
3. This Boston Red Sox "Splendid Splinter" often fished on New Brunswick's Miramichi River.
4. In which PEI community could you visit the Lucy Maud Montgomery Heritage Museum?
5. In 1822, this Englishman trekked across the island of Newfoundland with his Mi'kmaq guide.
6. In 1959, this Nova Scotia mining town became the first community to receive the Carnegie Medal.
7. A major lead and zinc deposit was discovered near this New Brunswick town in 1952.
8. The 1996 debut CD of this singer/songwriter from PEI is called *New Branches*.
9. What is the most northern cape in Newfoundland and Labrador?
10. The city of Sydney, Nova Scotia, is in which bay?

QUIZ #2

1. This New Brunswick community was named after James "Jock" Doyle.

2. This well-known poet from PEI was born at Charlottetown on March 30, 1923.

3. This Newfoundland river empties into the Bay of Islands near Corner Brook.

4. The team skipped by this champion female curler from Nova Scotia won the World Curling Championship in 2001.

5. In which New Brunswick city would you find Heritage Court?

6. This PEI community was originally called Grand River.

7. This well-known Newfoundland song by an unknown author was inducted into the Canadian Songwriters Hall of Fame in February 2005.

8. This Nova Scotia university had its beginnings as Horton Academy.

9. The first paid police force in Canada was established in this New Brunswick city in 1826.

10. This PEI-born singer created children's tunes such as "Cradle on the Waves."

QUIZ #3

1. Which Newfoundland politician wrote *My Years with Louis St. Laurent*?

2. Her novel *Pit Pony* was adapted as a TV series and film, which originally aired on CBC.

3. Who was the first governor of New Brunswick?

4. In which PEI community could you stand on Wood Islands Hill?

5. This actress from Newfoundland portrays Babe Bennett on *This Hour Has 22 Minutes*.

6. North America's first agricultural fair was held in this Nova Scotia community in 1752.

7. This was New Brunswick's first national park.

8. This Halifax newspaper was launched in 1974 and closed in 2008.

9. This governor of Harbour Grace, Newfoundland, wrote the first book of verse in North America.

10. The fleet of this wealthy privateer from Halifax helped Lord Nelson win the Battle of Trafalgar.

QUIZ #4

1. This New Brunswick theologian published *History, Prophecy and the Monuments* in three volumes.

2. In which PEI community could you visit A. A. Macdonald Gardens?

3. This Newfoundlander, author of *Will Anyone Search for Danny?*, was once the Canadian light heavyweight boxing champion.

4. This group won a 2003 ECMA for Best New Artists from the strength of their debut CD *Made in Cape Breton*.

5. This artist of such works as *Oxen with Red River Cart* died at Sussex, New Brunswick, in November 1889.

6. This unincorporated community on PEI was so named because its settlers from several nations co-existed peacefully.

7. This 1763 treaty gave Britain control over most of northern North America.

8. This NHL hockey player from Nova Scotia won the 2007 Lou Marsh Trophy as Canada's outstanding athlete.

9. These brothers started their potato-processing company at Florenceville, New Brunswick, in 1957.

10. This PEI community was originally called Carleton Point.

QUIZ #5

1. In St. John's, Newfoundland, what do the initials B. I. S. represent?

2. In 1975, this fourteen-year-old swimmer from Nova Scotia was named Canada's Female Athlete of the Year.

3. In which New Brunswick county would you find the community of St. George?

4. In 1986, this teacher founded the Institute of Island Studies at UPEI.

5. The name of this Newfoundland town may have come from the Spanish for "charcoal burners."

6. This fiddler from Mabou succeeded John Hamm as premier of Nova Scotia.

7. This New Brunswick woman was the first English Canadian to publish a novel in North America.

8. This area in Kings County, PEI, carries the name of old England.

9. What do Newfoundlanders call black, unsweetened tea?

10. Who wrote the books *Corporate Navigator: The Life of F. M. Covert* and the award-winning *An Illustrated History of Nova Scotia*?

QUIZ #6

1. This man developed such apple varieties as New Brunswick and Early Scarlet.

2. This unincorporated community in Prince County, PEI, was originally called Beaton Road.

3. The French had a colony at this "pleasant place" in Newfoundland.

4. In what year was Halifax founded?

5. This "one-man conglomerate" was born at Bouctouche, New Brunswick, in 1899.

6. In 2007, this singer from Iona, PEI, received her fifth consecutive East Coast Bluegrass Award for Female Vocalist of the Year.

7. This Newfoundland community was originally called Bird Island Cove.

8. Who succeeded Edgar Nelson Rhodes as premier of Nova Scotia?

9. The name of this New Brunswick park comes from the Maliseet for "big branch."

10. What is the third river that flows into Charlottetown Harbour other than the North (Yorke) and West (Eliot) rivers?

QUIZ #7

1. The Newfoundland and Labrador curling team led by this skip won a gold medal at the 2006 Winter Olympics in Turin, Italy.

2. In what year was Charlottetown incorporated?

3. This Moncton-based French-language daily newspaper published its last issue in 1982.

4. In 1972, Eldon officially became part of this PEI community.

5. In which Newfoundland community could you visit Commissariat House?

6. In the 1830s, this resident of Annapolis Royal became Nova Scotia's first policewoman.

7. This man from New Brunswick invented the steam foghorn in 1859.

8. This PEI locality got its name from the man who served as lieutenant-governor of the island from 1859 to 1868.

9. This aviator took off from Harbour Grace in 1932 and became the first woman to fly solo across the Atlantic Ocean.

10. He served as premier of colonial Nova Scotia from 1848 to 1854, making him the province's first premier.

QUIZ #8

1. Writer Antonine Maillet was born in this New Brunswick community.

2. This is the capital of Newfoundland and Labrador.

3. What was the main mineral mined at Tilt Cove, Newfoundland?

4. This Nova Scotia author won the 2001 Governor General's Award for poetry for *Execution Poems*.

5. Which New Brunswick postmaster-general put his own picture on an 1860 postage stamp?

6. Darnley became part of this PEI community in 1973.

7. This English captain was involved in the founding of the Society for Educating the Poor of Newfoundland in 1823.

8. This name given by the French to the Maritime region means "peaceful land."

9. This New Brunswick poet published a collection called *Smoked Glass* in 1977.

10. This unincorporated area of PEI was formerly called Pleasant Valley.

QUIZ #9

1. This Portuguese adventurer explored the area around Cape Race, Newfoundland, in 1520.
2. This Nova Scotia city was formerly called Chebucto.
3. Who succeeded Richard Hatfield as premier of New Brunswick?
4. His 2004 novel, *The Betrayer*, was based on a murder on PEI.
5. He was the first governor to spend a winter in Newfoundland.
6. Which author and illustrator team now residing in Nova Scotia collaborated on the award-winning children's book *Driftwood Cove*?
7. In 1875, this New Brunswick resident became the first Canadian woman to receive a university degree.
8. New Glasgow, PEI, sits on the banks of which river?
9. You can take the ferry to Nova Scotia from this port at the southwest corner of Newfoundland.
10. This Nova Scotia city has been called the "Birthplace of British Canada."

QUIZ #10

1. What is the capital of New Brunswick?

2. Thomas Douglas, known as Lord _____, sponsored displaced Scottish Highlanders in British colonies including PEI.

3. Which Newfoundland humorist and author wrote the song "The Squid-Jiggin' Ground"?

4. The name of this mythical Maritime creature means "man from nothing."

5. The name of this New Brunswick community comes from the French for "little house."

6. St. John's is located on the eastern side of this peninsula.

7. This English explorer was a half-brother of Sir Walter Raleigh's.

8. Who succeeded John Savage as premier of Nova Scotia?

9. In which New Brunswick county would you find the community of St. Martin's?

10. This unincorporated area of Queens County, PEI, was named in honour of a prominent British prime minister.

QUIZ #11

1. This is a craft where pieces of material are pulled through a stiff woven base such as burlap.

2. *Coal Fire in Winter*, an album by this well-known Cape Breton choir, was released in 1996.

3. This well-known soprano was born to Acadian parents at Timmins, Ontario, on April 25, 1946.

4. Who succeeded John A. Mathieson as premier of PEI?

5. This Newfoundland community was once called Jack of Clubs Cove.

6. This causeway links Cape Breton with mainland Nova Scotia.

7. In which New Brunswick community could you visit Queens County Museum?

8. A Christmas tree is sent to this American city each year in appreciation of the help given after the Halifax Explosion.

9. This broadcaster, well-known to Newfoundlanders, hosted TV programs such as *Where Once They Stood*.

10. Chignecto Bay is an indraft of which larger bay?

QUIZ #12

1. What is the name given to French-speaking residents of New Brunswick?

2. North River and Eliot River are part of this PEI town.

3. They were the first two women appointed to the Newfoundland cabinet after Confederation.

4. In 1995, this Nova Scotia singer/songwriter released the album *Return to the Cape*.

5. In 1686, this French engineer and cartographer mapped the Miramichi River and its tributaries.

6. This locality in Queens County, PEI, got its name from the homestead of Charles S. Parnell, former leader of the Irish Party.

7. Newfoundland's Trinity Bay Disaster of 1892 involved what annual spring activity?

8. In 2007, Halifax International Airport was named in honour of this twenty-second premier of Nova Scotia.

9. Who became premier of New Brunswick immediately after Bernard Lord?

10. This Newfoundland novelist wrote *The Colony of Unrequited Dreams*.

QUIZ #13

1. This name of Newfoundland's first major offshore oil field comes from an old name for Ireland.

2. The movie *Margaret's Museum* was based on his novel *The Glace Bay Miners' Museum*.

3. One of this artist's best-known works features a horse and a train.

4. Who succeeded Catherine Callbeck as premier of PEI?

5. What is the English translation of *Talamh an Éisc agus Labradóir*?

6. He succeeded Russell MacLellan as premier of Nova Scotia.

7. Who was the second premier of New Brunswick after Confederation?

8. Kathy Martin's 1981 book *Watershed Red* features this PEI river.

9. He became premier of Newfoundland and Labrador immediately after Clyde Wells.

10. The name of this Nova Scotia community comes from the Mi'kmaq for "red house."

QUIZ #14

1. This New Brunswick community is directly across the St. John River from Fort Kent, Maine.

2. This "new" bridge connects the north end of the Halifax peninsula with Dartmouth.

3. What is the largest natural lake on the island of Newfoundland?

4. What is the stage name of Cape Breton-born vocalist Richard Boudreau?

5. Bathurst, New Brunswick, is at the mouth of which river?

6. This legless stranger washed up on a Digby Neck beach in 1863.

7. This Newfoundland town on the Burin Peninsula was formerly called Mortier Bay.

8. Who was the subject of Brian Cuthbertson's *The Old Attorney General*, which was published in 1980?

9. Clement Moore, author of *The Night Before Christmas*, was the godson of this New Brunswick doctor, poet, and spy.

10. Inverness officially became part of which PEI community in 1983?

QUIZ #15

1. In 1927, this Italian navigator landed at Trepassey, Newfoundland, after circumnavigating the South Atlantic.

2. Will R. Bird's 1969 book, *An Earl Must Have a Wife*, deals with the life of this early governor of Cape Breton Island and PEI.

3. This self-educated geologist and paleontologist was born at Saint John, New Brunswick, in 1837.

4. This PEI community was originally called Portage.

5. In 1910, this author from Newfoundland published *Labrador: Its Discovery, Exploration and Development*.

6. This actress from Nova Scotia was nominated for an Oscar for her performance in the 2007 movie *Juno*.

7. What is the largest island in the Bay of Fundy?

8. This Newfoundland author wrote the award-winning novel *Down to the Dirt*.

9. Who was the first speaker of the Newfoundland House of Assembly?

10. This rock group, whose first single was "Fast Train," had its beginnings in Waverley, Nova Scotia, in 1969.

QUIZ #16

1. This resident of Fredericton, New Brunswick, was called "Canada's first father of pewtering."

2. This is the name that Jacques Cartier gave the Magdalen Islands when he arrived in 1534.

3. These islands to the south of Newfoundland are part of France.

4. This author won the 1997 Thomas Head Raddall Atlantic Fiction Award for his novel *Acadia*.

5. What is the longest river in New Brunswick?

6. In 2002, the PEI government appointed this man as the province's first poet laureate.

7. This movie about the seal hunt was the first sound film shot in Canada.

8. This Nova Scotia community was originally called McNair's Cove.

9. The Petitcodiac River flows into this northern arm of Chignecto Bay.

10. This tower was built to commemorate the 400th anniversary of Newfoundland's discovery by Europeans.

QUIZ #17

1. This American journalist and explorer died on an expedition in Labrador in October 1903.
2. This Nova Scotia community was once called Dorchester.
3. Who was the first premier of New Brunswick after Confederation?
4. The final book of poetry from this late poet is *Beautiful Veins*.
5. This community in Conception Bay, Newfoundland, was once called Turk's Gut.
6. Who founded Moirs, the future chocolatier, as a bakery at Halifax in 1815?
7. The McCain empire had its beginnings in this New Brunswick town.
8. The Anna Leonowens Gallery is associated with this university.
9. He was the first premier of the province of Newfoundland and Labrador.
10. This Nova Scotia community sits on the largest salt deposit in Atlantic Canada.

QUIZ #18

1. Who succeeded Frank McKenna as premier of New Brunswick?

2. The first play by this Newfoundland writer is *The Road Through Melton*.

3. In which Nova Scotia community could you tour the Wile Carding Mill?

4. This native leader, historian, and archaeologist was born at Big Cove, New Brunswick, in 1911.

5. The Hunter River is known by what name as it winds through New Glasgow, PEI?

6. This 1904 agreement between England and France resolved the French Shore dispute in Newfoundland.

7. This author, magician, and lecturer won the Evelyn Richardson Memorial Literary Award in 1982 for his book *Sable Island*.

8. This company, which produced a gull-winged car of the same name, went bankrupt in 1975.

9. In 1997, this singer, who grew up on PEI, became the first Canadian to win the Silver Pendant at Scotland's Royal Gaelic Mod.

10. This singer from Newfoundland won the Miss Dominion of Canada title in 1964.

QUIZ #19

1. Which strait separates Nova Scotia from PEI?

2. Novels by this famous New Brunswick author include *The Coming of Winter* and *Nights Below Station Street*.

3. Who took over from Keith Milligan as premier of PEI?

4. This American base was located near Quidi Vidi Lake in Newfoundland.

5. What is the name of the 1973 TV documentary that featured Dan R. MacDonald and other Cape Breton fiddlers?

6. Campbellton, New Brunswick, sits at the mouth of which river?

7. Maud Lewis' house is located in this art gallery.

8. This Newfoundlander became moderator of the United Church of Canada in 1964.

9. The community of Havre Boucher is in which Nova Scotia county?

10. Who succeeded John Baxter as premier of New Brunswick?

QUIZ #20

1. This PEI community was originally called Fyfe's Ferry.

2. The story of this woman's life is told in the book *Woman of Labrador*.

3. For many years, this Nova Scotia community was called "The Steel City."

4. This man from New Brunswick built Canada's first astronomical observatory.

5. Keppoch became part of which PEI community in 1995?

6. Which strait separates the island of Newfoundland from Labrador?

7. In 1940 this Nova Scotia resident became Canada's minister of munitions and supply.

8. The town of Plaster Rock is in which New Brunswick county?

9. This man from Summerside, PEI, became general manager of the NHL's Columbus Blue Jackets in 1998.

10. This renowned poet was born at Western Bay, Newfoundland, in 1882.

QUIZ #21

1. This community in Digby County, Nova Scotia, is named for the large clams found nearby.

2. Which province borders New Brunswick to the west?

3. This band is known for such albums as *Play* and *Sea of No Cares*.

4. The closest airport to Corner Brook, Newfoundland, is near which town?

5. This actress, born in Dartmouth, Nova Scotia, in 1910 starred in movies such as *42nd Street*.

6. In what year did New Brunswick celebrate its bicentennial?

7. Tyrone is part of which PEI municipality?

8. Kevin Blackmore, Wayne Chaulk, and Ray Johnson make up this zany group of entertainers from Newfoundland.

9. Early Acadians called this Nova Scotia community Les Planches.

10. In which New Brunswick community could you visit the Huntsman Marine Science Centre and Aquarium?

QUIZ #22

1. This community was the first capital of the colony of Nova Scotia.

2. This doctor administered the first smallpox vaccine in North America at Trinity, Newfoundland.

3. This director of movies such as *Fort Apache, the Bronx* was born in Glace Bay, Nova Scotia, in 1920.

4. This boxer from Baie St. Anne, New Brunswick, was nicknamed "The Fighting Fisherman."

5. He became premier of PEI in 1930 and again in 1935.

6. What was the nickname of the wooden coastal boats built at Clarenville, Newfoundland?

7. Jeffrey C. Domm's book *Ahmed and the Nest of Sand* features which shorebird?

8. A Celtic cross on this New Brunswick island pays tribute to Irish immigrants.

9. The community of Kensington is in which PEI county?

10. For many years, this Newfoundland journalist wrote the "Wayfarer" column in the *Daily News*.

QUIZ #23

1. *We Were Not the Savages*, by this native leader from Nova Scotia, was first published in 1993.

2. Which New Brunswick university is home to the Owens Art Gallery?

3. In what year did Jacques Cartier first arrive on PEI?

4. This lighthouse is a well-known landmark near the Newfoundland community of Twillingate.

5. This man who grew up in Hall's Harbour, Nova Scotia, helped reorganize the Turkish navy.

6. He served as premier of New Brunswick from 1878 to 1882.

7. Robert Allan Rankin's 1980 book *Down at the Shore* is a history of which PEI community?

8. The Newfoundland coat of arms features lions and which mythological animal?

9. This singer received the Juno Award for Best New Artist based on the success of her album *Adam's Rib*.

10. Parlee Beach is near which large New Brunswick town?

QUIZ #24

1. This Nova Scotia river gets its name from the Mi'kmaq for "great tidal river."

2. One of the plays written by this Newfoundlander is *As Loved Our Fathers*.

3. In 1782, women saved this Nova Scotia port from invading forces by reversing their scarlet-lined skirts to mimic a British regiment.

4. In 1923, this Miss Saint John became the first Miss Canada.

5. In 1867, William Annand took over from this man as premier of Nova Scotia.

6. What was Newfoundland's first national park?

7. This singer, called the "godfather of Celtic music," died on November 22, 2006.

8. This New Brunswick community is directly across the border from Van Buren, Maine.

9. This is Canada's oldest independent brewery.

10. This MP from St. John's West, Newfoundland, became Canada's minister of finance on June 4, 1979.

QUIZ #25

1. Michael MacDonald founded this, the oldest Scottish community on Cape Breton Island, in 1775.

2. Edmundston is located in this province.

3. Marq de Villiers' 2007 book, *Witch in the Wind*, presents the story of this famous schooner.

4. The Vikings established a settlement near this Newfoundland community around 1000 AD.

5. This contralto from Truro, Nova Scotia, made her stage debut in 1941.

6. The community of Chamcook is in which New Brunswick bay?

7. What is the meaning of the Mi'kmaq word *quoddy*?

8. This Newfoundland writer served as editor of the *Evening Telegram* from 1959 to 1982.

9. On February 23, 1909, J. A. D. McCurdy flew this craft over Baddeck Bay to make the first airplane flight in the British Empire.

10. Which New Brunswick city was once known as "The Bend"?

QUIZ #26

1. Who succeeded W. W. Sullivan as premier of PEI?

2. The defunct Advocate Mines open pit was near this Newfoundland community.

3. This enterprising Nova Scotia admiral was the subject of Julian Gwyn's 1974 book.

4. Poems by this New Brunswick author appeared in *Songs of the Common Day*.

5. Alaska is in which PEI county?

6. John White and Carol Brothers were regulars on this Newfoundland TV program.

7. This Nova Scotia community was once called Port Lomeron.

8. This New Brunswick community is home to the Shogomoc Historical and Model Railroad Club.

9. The Maritimes includes New Brunswick, Nova Scotia, and this province.

10. This Newfoundland captain led numerous Arctic expeditions for such explorers as Robert Peary and Vilhjalmur Stefansson.

QUIZ #27

1. This Nova Scotia community was originally called Horton's Corner.

2. This New Brunswick sea captain built Octagonal House, which now houses Sackville's Visitor Information Centre and Craft Gallery.

3. This PEI community once went by the name County Line.

4. What is the name for the sticks with their bark peeled off that were once used to make Newfoundland fishing flakes?

5. This beach near Lockeport, Nova Scotia, was featured on the Canadian fifty-dollar bill.

6. Oromocto is located in this province.

7. Who was the first woman elected to the Newfoundland legislature?

8. His song "Matthew's Voyage" was the official song of Nova Scotia's John Cabot five-hundredth anniversary celebrations.

9. An 1834 lithograph by this artist is titled *New Brunswick Fashionables*.

10. Melville became part of this PEI community in 1972.

QUIZ #28

1. Who wrote the Newfoundland song "The Kelligrews Soiree"?

2. This well-known actor and novelist was born at Halifax, Nova Scotia, on April 30, 1900.

3. This New Brunswick river gets its name from the Mi'kmaq for "a river that dashes roughly along."

4. The film *Mabel's Saga*, co-produced by this PEI film animator and the National Film Board, received several awards.

5. The Newfoundland community of Hampden is in which bay?

6. Antigonish, Nova Scotia, is the home of this well-known university.

7. Legend says that this earl discovered the Bay of Fundy in 1398.

8. This company is the world's largest producer of frozen french fries.

9. This Newfoundland fisherman is credited with leading archaeologists to the Viking site at L'Anse-aux-Meadows.

10. Nova Scotia's River Hebert empties into this ocean basin.

QUIZ #29

1. Who succeeded Camille Thériault as premier of New Brunswick in 1999?

2. Summerside, PEI, sits on an isthmus separating these two bays.

3. The name of this Newfoundland island is believed to have come from the Portuguese for "codfish."

4. Nova Scotia has this many seats in the House of Commons.

5. The community of Upsalquitch is in which New Brunswick county?

6. The name of this PEI community was selected in 1869 to replace the names Oyster Cove and Shipyard.

7. In 1892, this Englishman started his medical missionary practice in northern Newfoundland.

8. This man from Antigonish, Nova Scotia, became coach of the Toronto Maple Leafs in 1986.

9. In which New Brunswick bay would you find Portage Island?

10. This museum in southern Labrador was founded in 1978 and focuses on the contribution of local women.

QUIZ #30

1. He served as lieutenant-governor of Newfoundland from 1963 to 1969.

2. This Nova Scotia river was known to early Acadians as Rivière Rossignol.

3. He served as premier of New Brunswick from 1952 to 1960.

4. This Halifax-born singer founded the popular music festival Lilith Fair.

5. The Newfoundland community of Griquet is on which peninsula?

6. Alexander Keith's Brewery is best known for this kind of ale.

7. The Odell Park and Game Refuge is in which New Brunswick community?

8. This professional golfer from Charlottetown, PEI, joined the LPGA Tour in 1996.

9. Castle Hill National Historic Park is near which Newfoundland community?

10. This singer of "Seabird's Cry" starred in Eastern Front's *Stan Rogers: A Matter of Heart*.

QUIZ #31

1. This university has the only French-language law school in New Brunswick.

2. Georgetown, PEI, is at the mouth of which river?

3. Which former Newfoundland politician wrote the book *Dawn Without Light*?

4. The community of Arichat is in which Nova Scotia county?

5. Which New Brunswick community was originally called Nepisiguit?

6. This former mayor of Charlottetown served as lieutenant-governor of PEI from 1889 to 1894.

7. To an old-fashioned Newfoundlander, what is a lop?

8. This Maritime singer/songwriter released the album *When We Get There* in 2005.

9. From 1620 to 1621 New Brunswick was known by what name?

10. In 1986, this PEI-born TV journalist won an ACTRA award for his live coverage of the terrorist attack on the Turkish Embassy in Ottawa.

QUIZ # 32

1. Around one hundred people died in a fire at this St. John's hostel on December 12, 1942.

2. This CBC Television show about consumer awareness for teenagers was primarily based in Halifax.

3. This premier of British Columbia was born at Harvey, New Brunswick, in 1870.

4. This right-winger from PEI received the 1979 Lady Byng Memorial Trophy.

5. This famous explorer charted much of the Newfoundland coastline in the 1760s.

6. This TV journalist with the CBC was born at Antigonish, Nova Scotia, on January 7, 1964.

7. The town of Stanley is in which New Brunswick county?

8. The first issue of *The Beacon* was published in this PEI community in August 1992.

9. This ocean current flows south along the coast of Newfoundland.

10. Who was the last colonial premier of Nova Scotia?

QUIZ # 33

1. This notorious American deserter settled in New Brunswick in 1785.
2. Tradition holds that this PEI community gets its name from early French settler Rene Rassicot.
3. Which Newfoundland politician compiled the multi-volume series *The Book of Newfoundland*?
4. This community in Pictou County, Nova Scotia, is named for the governor general of Canada from 1872 to 1878.
5. Pascal Poirier House is in which New Brunswick community?
6. In 1907, this Biblical scholar and academic from PEI became president of the University of Toronto.
7. Near which Newfoundland cape could you watch waves wash into "The Dungeon"?
8. Who became premier of Nova Scotia immediately after G. I. Smith?
9. This New Brunswick community was once called Leger Corner.
10. The province of Newfoundland and Labrador has this many seats in the House of Commons.

QUIZ # 34

1. This well-known Newfoundland fiddler was born at Daniel's Harbour in 1899.

2. The Nova Scotia village of Grand Pré is featured in this classic Longfellow epic.

3. This native of Andover, New Brunswick, became ambassador to Ireland in 1976.

4. St. Eleanors became part of which PEI community in 1995?

5. What was the former name of the Newfoundland community of Valley Pond?

6. A truck driver stole over 50,000 cans of this beer bound for Mexico in August 2004.

7. Beaubears Island is on which New Brunswick river?

8. In 1989, he skipped the PEI team to the Canadian Mixed Curling Championship.

9. This street that runs parallel to Water Street in St. John's is named for a Newfoundland governor.

10. Her 1999 poetry collection, *The Bridge That Carries the Road*, was nominated for a Governor General's Award.

QUIZ # 35

1. The Innu are indigenous people of Quebec and
   _____.

2. The village of Bonshaw is in which PEI county?

3. For many years, this man, born in Petty Harbour, Newfoundland, kept detailed records of the annual seal hunt.

4. She was the leader of the NDP of Nova Scotia from 1981 to 1994 and the federal NDP from 1995 to 2003.

5. The name of this New Brunswick community comes from the Maliseet for "deep water."

6. This war photographer from PEI was born September 24, 1889.

7. Who was the last prime minister of Newfoundland before Confederation?

8. The name of this Nova Scotia port comes from the Mi'kmaq for "seal-hunting place."

9. One of the books by this New Brunswick writer books is called *Stilt Jack*.

10. This New Brunswick-born actor starred in such movies as *Casanova* and *Eye of the Needle*.

QUIZ # 36

1. You can take a ferry from this northeast Newfoundland port to Happy Valley, Labrador.

2. The second floor of the Maritime Museum of the Atlantic is dedicated to this shipping line.

3. Who succeeded John McNair as premier of New Brunswick?

4. Natives called this PEI river *Pogoosumkek-seboo*.

5. This Newfoundland activist started the Fishermen's Protective Union.

6. Michael R. Welton's biography of this labour organizer is called *Little Mosie from the Margaree*.

7. Which New Brunswick community was once called Osnaburg?

8. This film festival is held every September in Halifax, Nova Scotia.

9. The island of Merasheen is in which Newfoundland bay?

10. This river in Antigonish County, Nova Scotia, was formerly called Little River.

QUIZ # 37

1. The Marjorie Young Bell Conservatory of Music is part of which New Brunswick university?

2. What is the real name of hip-hop artist Buck 65?

3. This Norwegian worked with her husband to unearth the history of L'Anse-aux-Meadows, Newfoundland.

4. This community in Cape Breton County, Nova Scotia, was once called Old Bridgeport.

5. This New Brunswick governor tossed dice with his brother over the claim to most of Madawaska County.

6. Natives called this PEI promontory *Setunook*.

7. This 1783 treaty gave France the right to fish along the west coast of Newfoundland.

8. Pier __ is known as Canada's Immigration Museum.

9. What was the original name of the University of New Brunswick?

10. This artist designed Our Island Home, an interactive museum at PEI's Gateway Village.

QUIZ # 38

1. What industrial activity is celebrated in the Newfoundland song "The Badger Drive"?

2. This former premier of Nova Scotia became the fourth prime minister of Canada.

3. In 2000, he became the first New Brunswick athlete to win a gold medal at the Paralympic Games.

4. PEI's Jacques River flows west into this bay.

5. Cabot Tower sits atop which famous Newfoundland hill?

6. This "old" bridge connects the Halifax peninsula with Dartmouth and first opened in 1955.

7. This New Brunswick lumber baron set up the first commercial salmon fishery on the Miramichi River.

8. Upton became part of this PEI community in 1975.

9. He became prime minister of Newfoundland in 1919 and again in 1928.

10. This Nova Scotia port was once called Chebec.

QUIZ # 39

1. The New Brunswick community of St. George is in which bay?

2. The Acadian flag features these four colours.

3. Explorer Jacques Cartier called this Newfoundland port St. Catherine's Haven.

4. This woman from Nova Scotia founded the Comfort Heart Initiative.

5. Which New Brunswick logging town claims to have the world's largest axe?

6. Hit songs by this PEI singer/songwriter include "Evidence" and "If I Fall."

7. This pirate took over Newfoundland forts abandoned by Peter Easton.

8. This is the former name of the Rooms Provincial Art Gallery.

9. In which New Brunswick community could you visit Sainte-Anne-du-Bocage Shrine?

10. The 2000 book *Along Lot Seven Shore* deals with the folk songs and writings of these three brothers from PEI.

QUIZ # 40

1. What do Newfoundlanders call the ledge of ice frozen along the shoreline?

2. This man from Clark's Harbour, Nova Scotia, is credited with designing the Cape Island boat.

3. This university has the only English-language law school in New Brunswick.

4. This community in Prince County, PEI, was once called Hawthorne.

5. This Newfoundland musical duo had a major hit with "The Mummers' Song."

6. The name of this small community in Inverness County comes from the Mi'kmaq for "place where two rivers meet."

7. From 1691 to 1696 New Brunswick was known by this name.

8. This multi-faceted artist from PEI published *And My Name is... Stories from the Quilt* in 2006.

9. This is the only province that shares a land border with Newfoundland and Labrador.

10. This is the indoor amusement park located in Dieppe, New Brunswick.

QUIZ # 41

1. The New Brunswick community of Florenceville is named after this person.

2. Foxley River is located in this province.

3. This politician from Bell Island once served as leader of the Newfoundland Liberal Party.

4. Deanne Fitzpatrick, author of *Hook Me a Story*, practises this art.

5. Which New Brunswick community is home to MacDonald Farm Historic Site?

6. This is the longest river in Nova Scotia.

7. Fort Frederick was part of which Newfoundland historic site?

8. She was born in Inverness County, Nova Scotia, in 1972, and is one of the best-known musicians of Cape Breton fiddle music.

9. Who was the first lieutenant-governor of New Brunswick after Confederation?

10. This PEI cape was once called Eglington Point.

QUIZ # 42

1. What do Newfoundlanders call a homemade grapnel consisting of a wooden frame around a stone?

2. In the 1890s work began on this never-completed railway between Tidnish, Nova Scotia, and the Bay of Fundy.

3. Judith Hoegg Ryan's book *Coal in Our Blood* deals with two hundred years of coal mining in this Nova Scotia county.

4. Elizabeth Irving called this New Brunswick artist "Painter and Man of God."

5. Woody Point is in which Newfoundland bay?

6. Neil Robinson's 1997 book, *To the Ends of the Earth*, tells the story of this preacher who moved with his clan from Nova Scotia to New Zealand.

7. Who became premier of New Brunswick immediately after James Murray?

8. Rosebank Point extends into this PEI port.

9. This CBC TV personality from Newfoundland was a host of *This Hour Has 22 Minutes* before launching his own show.

10. Which island off Nova Scotia has been called "The Graveyard of the Atlantic"?

QUIZ # 43

1. This New Brunswick mountain is the highest in the Maritimes.

2. In 2005, this former lieutenant-governor of PEI published the book *These Roots Run Deep*.

3. What is the official flower of Newfoundland and Labrador?

4. This island near Baddeck was formerly called Duffus Island.

5. In the 1630s, this French adventurer built a fort at Portland Point, New Brunswick.

6. PEI's Dock River flows south into this bay.

7. This English explorer led an expedition up the Exploits River in 1810–1811 in search of the Beothuk.

8. A. J. B. Johnston's 2007 book, *Endgame 1758*, features this historic Nova Scotia settlement.

9. This Fredericton church claims to have the first new cathedral foundation built on British soil after the Norman Conquest.

10. Haliburton is in which PEI county?

QUIZ # 44

1. This Scottish-born woman served as secretary of the Newfoundland Historical Society for twenty years.

2. This TV journalist, known for *The Fifth Estate*, wrote *Causeway: A Passage from Innocence*.

3. This paleontologist from Saint John, New Brunswick, was the second woman to be elected a fellow of the Royal Society of Canada.

4. Who succeeded Aubin Arsenault as premier of PEI?

5. In which port could you visit the Southern Newfoundland Seamen's Museum?

6. This Canadian politician and brewmaster from Nova Scotia was born in 1795.

7. The New Brunswick community of Dalhousie is in which county?

8. This is the second largest city in Atlantic Canada.

9. What was the original name of world-famous Newfoundland-born opera singer Marie Toulinguet?

10. These "public gardens" are located at the corner of Spring Garden Road and South Park Street in this city.

QUIZ # 45

1. This New Brunswick city was the first city to be incorporated in Canada.

2. This famous mariner was born at Mount Hanley, Nova Scotia, on February 20, 1844.

3. What is the longest river in the province of Newfoundland and Labrador?

4. This barque, which was overrun by mutiny and piracy, was shipwrecked on the eastern shore of Nova Scotia in 1844.

5. In which New Brunswick city could you meet friends at the Free Meeting House?

6. In 1945, this Charlottetown-born man was awarded the Medal of Honor by US President Harry S. Truman.

7. Who was the first prime minister of Newfoundland?

8. This community in Antigonish County, Nova Scotia, was once called Rear Malignant Cove.

9. What Latin phrase appears on the New Brunswick coat of arms?

10. This is the only Atlantic province with no natural dry-land connection to the rest of Canada.

QUIZ # 46

1. What is a *komatik*?

2. This *Hockey Night in Canada* announcer was born in Sydney, Nova Scotia, on April 11, 1917.

3. A New Brunswick ballad tells the story of this young man fatally injured in the Miramichi woods.

4. The locality of Monticello is in which PEI county?

5. Who wrote *The Ode to Newfoundland*?

6. Boar's Head Lighthouse is on which Nova Scotia island?

7. This New Brunswick city began as the French community of Ste. Anne's Point.

8. This is the smallest province in terms of both size and population.

9. The Labrador port of Cartwright is in which bay?

10. Nova Scotia is Latin for ___ _____.

QUIZ # 47

1. This New Brunswicker once owned one of the largest cotton mills in the country, which was located in Marysville.

2. The native name for this PEI beach is *Penamkeak*.

3. What is the name of the cross on the Newfoundland coat of arms?

4. This community in Antigonish County, Nova Scotia, was once called Back Settlement of Harbour Bouche.

5. New Brunswick has this many seats in the House of Commons.

6. The village of Alexandra is in which PEI county?

7. This southpaw held the Newfoundland bantamweight title for ten years and represented Newfoundland at the 1930 British Empire Games.

8. Caroline Stellings' book *The Malagawatch Mice and the Church that Sailed* tells the story of how the Malagawatch Church was floated across this body of water in Nova Scotia.

9. This British army officer built New Brunswick's Fort Frederick.

10. This politician coined the term "Atlantic Canada" when Newfoundland joined Canada.

QUIZ # 48

1. What is the name for an Inuit canoe covered with sealskin?

2. This country music singer, also known as Fred Lays, hails from New Glasgow, Nova Scotia.

3. The name of this marsh near the Nova Scotia–New Brunswick border comes from the French for "din."

4. Charlottetown's Joey Kitson is a member of this musical group.

5. This American wrote *Vikings of the Ice*, which was published in 1924.

6. She was the host of the CBC Television show *Rita and Friends*.

7. This outspoken president of Canada's PC Party was born at Woodstock, New Brunswick, in 1920.

8. The locality of Victoria Cross is in which PEI county?

9. The Latin *Terra Nova* refers to this province.

10. The Victorian, one of Canada's first automobiles, was manufactured in this Nova Scotia community in 1898.

QUIZ # 49

1. This city preceded Fredericton as the capital of New Brunswick.

2. PEI's Midgell River flows north into this bay.

3. This northern Newfoundland town was the headquarters of the Grenfell Mission.

4. Who succeeded William Young as premier of the colony of Nova Scotia?

5. This New Brunswick community is home to College St-Louis Maillet.

6. This premier of PEI was born at Central Bedeque on July 25, 1939.

7. This Newfoundlander, born in 1757, became known as "Prince of the Hebrews."

8. This artist and naturalist won the 2006 Evelyn Richardson Prize for Non-fiction for *Birds of a Feather: Tales of a Wild Bird Haven*.

9. A statue of this Scottish poet looks toward New Brunswick's Legislative Building.

10. The Newfoundland community of Burnside is on which peninsula?

QUIZ # 50

1. *Sailors, Slackers and Blind Pigs: Halifax at War*, by this award-winning author, was published in 2002.

2. The Saint John and Nashwaaksis rivers meet at this New Brunswick city.

3. What is the capital of PEI?

4. This New Brunswick-born singer sold over three million copies of the album *Hélène*.

5. This artist and publisher, born in Northampton, England, received the 1999 Adrien Arsenault Senior Arts Award for her contribution to the arts on PEI.

6. This speed skater from Saint John, New Brunswick, became known as "the man with the million-dollar legs."

7. These people are the first inhabitants of PEI.

8. What do Newfoundlanders call the covered space at the front of a boat?

9. This rock band from Nova Scotia released the album *Between the Bridges* in 1999.

10. This man was the last French governor of Acadia.

QUIZ # 51

1. In which PEI community could you take in a hockey game at Jacques Cartier Memorial Arena?

2. What was the common name of the early Newfoundland colonist who became the first Lord Baltimore?

3. This CTV journalist has hosted *Christmas Daddies* for over twenty-five years.

4. The New Brunswick community of Saint-Antoine is in which county?

5. This PEI community was once called Groshaut Settlement.

6. In what year was Newfoundland's Confederation Building first completed?

7. This accomplished composer and flautist was born at Kentville, Nova Scotia, on August 28, 1939.

8. This New Brunswick community has been called the "Brussels Sprouts Capital of Canada."

9. Breadalbane is located in this province.

10. Newfoundland's Bay of Exploits is part of which larger bay?

QUIZ # 52

1. These Halifax brothers released the album *Sailor's Story* in 2000.

2. The town of Rexton, New Brunswick, is near the mouth of which river?

3. This publisher and writer won the 2003 Ann Connor Brimer Children's Literature Prize for *Shoulder the Sky*.

4. The Newfoundland Beothuk tribe was part of which native group?

5. The town of Bible Hill is in which Nova Scotia county?

6. This woman from Shediac, New Brunswick, became the first female Speaker of the Canadian Senate.

7. This community in Kings County, PEI, was once called Indian Town Road.

8. The Cantwell family tended the lighthouse at this Newfoundland cape for many years.

9. Angus L. Macdonald was born in this community in Inverness County, Nova Scotia, in 1890.

10. Who wrote the book *River Boy: Life along the St. John*?

QUIZ # 53

1. The village of Darlington is in which PEI county?

2. This native of the Azores was reportedly John Cabot's pilot in 1498.

3. John Johnston's 2004 book, subtitled *Heart of Acadie*, features this Nova Scotia community.

4. Fort Beausejour is near which New Brunswick city?

5. This hurricane hit Atlantic Canada in September 2003 and left extensive damage across Nova Scotia and PEI.

6. This river flows through Glenwood, Newfoundland.

7. This is the only national park that is also a national historic site.

8. This New Brunswick community claims to have the largest sardine factory in the British Commonwealth.

9. The village of O'Leary is in which PEI county?

10. This Newfoundland singer became known for her rendition of "Thank God We're Surrounded By Water."

QUIZ # 54

1. This Nova Scotia community was once called Albion Mines.

2. Father of Confederation William Henry Steeves was born in this New Brunswick community.

3. This mountain range extends into the Atlantic provinces.

4. John Guy founded this Newfoundland "Valentine Town" in 1610.

5. This hockey player, born in Port Hood, Nova Scotia, played twenty-three seasons in the NHL.

6. This New Brunswick city has been called the "Pewtersmith Capital of Canada."

7. This is Mi'kmaq History Month.

8. This Newfoundlander's team won the Labatt Brier curling championship in 1976.

9. Who wrote the book *Before Green Gables*?

10. This woman from Dieppe, New Brunswick, was enrolled in the Order of Canada for her work with hundreds of unwanted foster children.

QUIZ # 55

1. Her second album, *Church Bell Blues*, won four awards at the 2006 Music PEI Awards.

2. To a Newfoundlander, what is a dwye?

3. This former leader of Canada's peacekeeping forces in Bosnia hails from Truro, Nova Scotia.

4. This whirlpool near Deer Island, New Brunswick, is reportedly the second largest in the world.

5. This area of PEI got its Biblical name from James Douglas, a Sunday school teacher.

6. Who was the first Newfoundland governor to live in the present Government House?

7. She won the 2006 Thomas Head Raddall Atlantic Fiction Award for her novel *Sylvanus Now*.

8. This was the first feature film produced in New Brunswick.

9. The village of Richmond is in which PEI county?

10. What is the common name for *Sterna paradisaea*?

QUIZ # 56

1. What do you call a resident of Labrador?

2. In which New Brunswick community could you visit the Lutz Mountain Heritage Museum?

3. This soccer player from Charlottetown, PEI, signed a contract with the Toronto Lynx in 2006.

4. Who served as lieutenant-governor of Newfoundland from 1981 to 1986?

5. One of this Nova Scotian songwriter's compositions was "Song for the Mira."

6. The Bell Inn, the oldest stone building in New Brunswick, is located in this community.

7. McCallum's Point extends into this PEI bay.

8. This Newfoundland humorist won the Stephen Leacock Memorial Medal for *That Far Greater Bay*.

9. This community in Antigonish County, Nova Scotia, was once called Yankee Grant.

10. One of this nineteenth-century artist's watercolours is titled *Travelling on the River St. John, New Brunswick*.

QUIZ # 57

1. Kent Macdonald's book *From a Distance* features this island off Georgetown, PEI.

2. What was the first ship in Newfoundland's Alphabet Fleet?

3. In 2003, this fiddler from Judique released the album *Cape Breton Tradition*.

4. The summer cottage of Sir William Cornelius Van Horne is located on Minister's Island outside of this New Brunswick town.

5. This mountain in Labrador is the highest point in mainland Canada east of the Rockies.

6. How does one say Newfoundland and Labrador in French?

7. This Nova Scotia author's 1995 book, *The Lie That Had To Be*, was nominated for several awards.

8. This Loyalist soldier led the New Brunswick Fencibles during the War of 1812.

9. The village of Burlington is in which PEI county?

10. Cassie Brown's *A Winter's Tale* tells the story of the wreck of this ship off Newfoundland in 1918.

QUIZ # 58

1. This Nova Scotia resident's 1984 novel *Book of Fears* was short-listed for the Governor General's Award.

2. This island in the Bay of Fundy is home to nine hundred pairs of breeding Atlantic puffins.

3. This actress from Charlottetown, PEI, starred as the title character in the TV series *The Trouble With Tracy*.

4. Williamsport, Newfoundland, was a major centre for which marine industry?

5. In which province can you find Cape Enrage?

6. Which American president had a vacation home on Campobello Island?

7. In which PEI community is the International Fox Museum?

8. What do Newfoundlanders mean by the term "duckish"?

9. This river runs through the community of Weymouth Falls, Nova Scotia.

10. In 1851, this sailing ship from New Brunswick made the round trip from Britain to Australia in record time.

QUIZ # 59

1. Charlottetown's Chris Murphy is a member of this rock band.

2. This Newfoundland community was once called Wellington.

3. From 1955 to 1970, this zoologist, born in Kentville, Nova Scotia, served as chief curator of zoology at Chicago's Field Museum.

4. This New Brunswick poet was one of Canada's best-known poets during his lifetime and he wrote *Low Tide on the Grand Pré: A Book of Lyrics*.

5. The village of Miminegash is in which PEI county?

6. Who founded the Newfoundland Teachers' Association?

7. *Le Petit Acadien*, by this author from Nova Scotia, was published in 1979.

8. The members of this New Brunswick team were Canada's senior hockey champs from 1932 to 1934.

9. The Charlottetown estate known as Ardgowan was the home of this Father of Confederation.

10. This sergeant from White Bay, Newfoundland, received the Victoria Cross in 1919.

QUIZ # 60

1. The community of Berwick is in which Nova Scotia county?

2. This financier and industrialist was born at Bathurst, New Brunswick, on October 29, 1874.

3. This artist, born in PEI's Wilmot Valley in the nineteenth century, became known for her miniature portraits and still lifes on small pieces of ivory.

4. This newspaper was published at Twillingate, Newfoundland, for many years.

5. This native poet from Nova Scotia published *Song of Eskasoni* in 1988.

6. This 1842 treaty settled the boundary dispute between New Brunswick and Maine.

7. As the name suggests, three plagues of mice invaded this PEI community between 1720 and 1738.

8. Pirate Peter Easton had his headquarters in this Newfoundland port.

9. This is the most populous province in Atlantic Canada.

10. In which New Brunswick community could you visit Williston House?

QUIZ # 61

1. St. Anthony, Newfoundland, is in which bay?
2. This merchant mariner from New Glasgow won the Canadian Junior Lightweight boxing title on June 30, 1964.
3. His novel about the American Revolution is titled *Barbara Ladd*.
4. The village of Morell is in which PEI county?
5. On December 2, 1901, this Italian received the first transatlantic message atop Signal Hill, St. John's, Newfoundland.
6. This author from Nova Scotia won the 2004 Griffin Poetry Prize for *Loop*.
7. Natives called this rock near Grand Manan *Menaskook*.
8. This radical poet from PEI helped found the "underground" newspaper *Georgia Strait*.
9. This Newfoundland premier was born at Gambo.
10. John Maxwell's 1979 book features this floating abandoned ship of the same name.

QUIZ # 62

1. This actor, who starred in the wartime classic *Mrs. Miniver*, was born at Saint John, New Brunswick, on September 23, 1897.

2. The locality of Woodstock is in which PEI county?

3. This annual boat-racing event in St. John's, Newfoundland, began in the 1820s.

4. *Surfacing*, the bestselling album by this singer from Nova Scotia, won four Junos and two Grammy Awards.

5. New Brunswick's first nuclear power station was built here.

6. This hockey defenceman from Charlottetown was drafted by the Boston Bruins in 1970.

7. What is the largest community on Bell Island?

8. The name of this Nova Scotia community comes from the Scottish Gaelic for "mountain of birds."

9. This Halifax rock musician was the lead singer of Thrush Hermit and released the solo album *La De Da*.

10. Panmure Head extends into which PEI bay?

QUIZ # 63

1. This Memorial University professor wrote a two-volume biography of poet E. J. Pratt.
2. This former mayor of Dartmouth became premier of Nova Scotia in 1993.
3. The name of this New Brunswick bay comes from the Mi'kmaq for "a bay that turns back on itself."
4. This is the easternmost point in Canada.
5. This became Newfoundland's official flag in 1952.
6. This community in Cumberland County, Nova Scotia, was previously called Mill Village.
7. This king of France donated the bell for the chapel at Meductic, New Brunswick.
8. How does one say Nova Scotia in French?
9. This passenger ferry sank off the coast of Labrador on June 2, 1977.
10. Kentville, Nova Scotia, is located in this county.

QUIZ # 64

1. In which New Brunswick community could you visit the Atlantic Salmon Museum?

2. In 1998, this inspirational group from PEI released the album *Confederation Bridge*.

3. Which Newfoundland author wrote the novel *River Thieves*?

4. Which Nova Scotia community was once called Habitant Corner?

5. The *Daily Gleaner* is the newspaper of which New Brunswick community?

6. The national headquarters of this federal department moved to Charlottetown in 1983.

7. You can visit a Maritime Archaic Indian burial site near this community on Newfoundland's Great Northern Peninsula.

8. This author from Nova Scotia won the 1996 Ann Connor Brimer Children's Literature Prize for his book, *Of Things Not Seen*.

9. New Brunswick was once part of which province?

10. What is the postal abbreviation for Prince Edward Island?

QUIZ # 65

1. All hands were lost when this sealing ship sank off Newfoundland around March 31, 1914.

2. The community of Chignecto is in which Nova Scotia county?

3. He served as premier of New Brunswick from 1900 to 1907.

4. Loyalist became part of this PEI community in 1974.

5. This Newfoundland-born actor starred as *Quentin Durgens, M. P.*

6. The community of Dagger Woods is in which Nova Scotia county?

7. This New Brunswick poet received the Evelyn Richardson Memorial Literary Award for *Double Exposure*.

8. Pownal Bay, PEI, is on the north shore of which larger bay?

9. This Newfoundland town was named after the Duke of Clarence.

10. *Guardian of the Gulf*, by Brian Tennyson and Roger Sarty, recounts the role of this Nova Scotia port in North Atlantic military strategy.

QUIZ # 66

1. Where is the Mines and Minerals Interpretation Centre of New Brunswick?

2. One of the songs by this farmer/songwriter from PEI is called "The Potato Bug."

3. The Newfoundland community of Herring Neck is on which island?

4. This hockey player from Halifax, Nova Scotia, was picked by the Boston Bruins in 1991.

5. This New Brunswick community is considered the capital of the Republic of Madawaska.

6. This novel written by Frank Parker Day won CBC Radio's *Canada Reads* competition in 2005.

7. What name was given to fishermen who lived in Labrador during the summer months?

8. In 1992, this jazz singer from Nova Scotia released the album *Blame It on My Youth*.

9. North Head is on which New Brunswick island?

10. This tidal phenomenon occurs in the Petitcodiac River of New Brunswick and the Shubenacadie River of Nova Scotia.

QUIZ # 67

1. Around 1500, King Manuel of Portugal gave this explorer a charter to claim lands in North America.

2. The only two medical schools in Atlantic Canada are located in Nova Scotia and this province.

3. This New Brunswick river has been called "The Rhine of North America."

4. New Zealand is part of which PEI county?

5. Which well-known journalist wrote the book *Smallwood: The Unlikely Revolutionary*?

6. The name of this community in Kings County, Nova Scotia, comes from the French for "alewife."

7. The Charlotte County Museum is located in the historic home of this New Brunswick man.

8. This nurse from PEI, who served in World War I, earned the nickname "Bird."

9. The Newfoundland community of Bell Island is in which bay?

10. The Oland family opened their first brewery in this province.

QUIZ # 68

1. This New Brunswick community joined with Riverview in 1973.

2. In 1993, this comedienne from PEI released the collection *Pumping Irony*.

3. This journalist from Newfoundland began hosting CBC Radio's *Cross Country Checkup* in 1994.

4. The community of Eskasoni is in which Nova Scotia county?

5. This lumber boss led a private army into Maine and was later elected to the New Brunswick legislature.

6. The locality of Suffolk is in which PEI county?

7. This flightless bird, which lived on Funk Island, Newfoundland, became extinct in 1844.

8. This is the largest town on the South Shore of Nova Scotia.

9. This New Brunswick community features a replica of the shrine at Lourdes, France.

10. This rock group, well-known in the 1980s and '90s, received the 2006 Music PEI Lifetime Achievement Award.

QUIZ # 69

1. What is the name for a waterproof fisherman's hat?

2. *Trailer Park Boys* creator Mark Clattenburg and actors Robb Wells and John Paul Tremblay hail from this community near Halifax.

3. This southeast New Brunswick dish is made from grated potatoes, flour, and meat.

4. This explorer wrote *Through Trackless Labrador* about his journey in the early 1900s.

5. Which Newfoundland humorist wrote the pieces in *Tales from Pigeon Inlet*?

6. The community of Cheticamp is in which Nova Scotia county?

7. This New Brunswick professor wrote the novels *The Dodge Club* and *A Strange Manuscript Found in a Copper Cylinder*.

8. PEI's Fox River flows northeast into which port?

9. What was the first steamship to visit Newfoundland?

10. Royal Doulton's dinner pattern "Blossom Time" depicts May blossoms of this Nova Scotia valley.

QUIZ # 70

1. The name of this New Brunswick community comes from the Mi'kmaq for "running far back."

2. In 1986, he became the twenty-ninth premier of PEI.

3. This community in Labrador was originally called Carol Lake.

4. This hockey player from Kentville, Nova Scotia, was drafted by the Minnesota North Stars in 1972.

5. This New Brunswick man was captain of the *Marco Polo* when it made a record trip from England to Australia and back in 1852.

6. This New Brunswick river is nicknamed "Chocolate River."

7. This pirate held Newfoundland Governor Richard Whitbourne hostage for eleven weeks.

8. What was the unofficial name given to the blizzard that struck Atlantic Canada the winter following Hurricane Juan?

9. What is the official flower of New Brunswick?

10. This PEI-born singer/songwriter, popular in Quebec, received the Order of Canada in 2003.

QUIZ # 71

1. She wrote *The Victory of Geraldine Gull*.

2. This community in Antigonish County was once called "the back settlement of Knoydart."

3. This man from Newcastle, New Brunswick, was Canada's first minister of fisheries.

4. Tracadie is in which PEI county?

5. What is the more common name for a sea parrot?

6. Alan Villiers' 1953 book about this famous ship is subtitled *Last of a Glorious Era*.

7. Magnetic Hill is near which New Brunswick city?

8. Eastern Canada includes Atlantic Canada plus these two provinces.

9. He served as lieutenant-governor of Newfoundland from 1969 to 1974.

10. *Love and Death on Long Island* is one of many films shot in and around this Nova Scotia port.

QUIZ # 72

1. What is the English translation of Baie Des Chaleurs?

2. This Nova Scotia town is well-known for sailing and has two natural harbours, Front Harbour and Back Harbour.

3. What does the Newfoundland word "fousty" mean?

4. This actor, born in Kentville, Nova Scotia, starred in movies such as *The Game* and *The China Syndrome*.

5. This New Brunswick community got its name from a major in the famous 104th Regiment.

6. This river separates St. Stephen, New Brunswick, from Calais, Maine.

7. This Newfoundland-born boxer won both the American and World heavyweight boxing titles in 1879.

8. This cape in Antigonish County, Nova Scotia, was known to early French explorers as Cap St. Louis.

9. Who was the second Acadian lieutenant-governor of New Brunswick?

10. Kinlock became part of this PEI community in 1995.

QUIZ # 73

1. The *Gil Eannes* was the hospital ship for this foreign fishing fleet, which often visited St. John's, Newfoundland.

2. *Eilean Cheap Breatuinn* is Scottish Gaelic for this island.

3. In which New Brunswick city could you take in performances at the Playhouse?

4. This Charlottetown-born producer and director became director of Canada's National Theatre School in 1987.

5. This Newfoundland community was formerly called Gayside.

6. This noted clergyman and linguist was born near Kentville, Nova Scotia, on May 18, 1810.

7. What is the common name for *Matteuccia struthiopteris*?

8. Surrey became part of this PEI community in 1972.

9. This missionary doctor brought a herd of reindeer to Newfoundland in 1906.

10. This author, known for his syndicated "Crime Flashback" column, was born in Antigonish, Nova Scotia, in 1931.

QUIZ # 74

1. Natives called this New Brunswick community Telakadik.

2. In 1909, this man from Charlottetown, PEI, published the novel *The Inner Shrine*.

3. What was the nickname of the train that travelled across Newfoundland for more than seventy years?

4. This outspoken member of Parliament was born at Amherst, Nova Scotia, on February 19, 1945.

5. This New Brunswick river gets its name from the Mi'kmaq for "good river."

6. In 1999, this step-dancing fiddler from PEI released the album *Come Dance With Me*.

7. Who was the second prime minister of Newfoundland?

8. Who is the vocalist on Ashley MacIsaac's 1995 hit single "Sleepy Maggie"?

9. This son of a New England judge was held captive at Meductic, New Brunswick, for six years.

10. Courtin Island is in this PEI bay.

QUIZ # 75

1. For many years this white ship served as a floating TB clinic for many Newfoundland outports.

2. Where is the Great Hall of the Clans Museum?

3. This New Brunswick river was once called Rivière des Barques.

4. This MP from PEI was appointed Canada's minister of the environment in 1985.

5. One of this Newfoundland realist painter's works is *Salmon Between Two Sinks*.

6. Joggin Bridge is in which Nova Scotia county?

7. This journalist and politician started publishing the *Saint John Weekly Freeman* in 1849.

8. This PEI community is sometimes called the "Gateway to Îles de Madeleine."

9. He became prime minister of Newfoundland on March 7, 1900.

10. This college is located in Bible Hill, Nova Scotia.

QUIZ # 76

1. What is the name of Moncton's AHL team?

2. In 1979, this clergyman from PEI became secretary of state for Canada in the short-lived Joe Clark government.

3. This monthly paper, first published in January 1924, gave "all the news from all over Newfoundland."

4. In 1975, this poet published *The Cape Breton Book of the Dead*.

5. The first lighthouse in New Brunswick was erected on this island near Saint John in 1791.

6. In 2004, this hockey player from Murray Harbour, PEI, received both the Conn Smythe and Lady Byng trophies.

7. Joe Batt's Arm is in which Newfoundland bay?

8. Sydney County, Nova Scotia, was given what new name in 1863?

9. This New Brunswick professor and poet edited *The Fiddlehead* from 1952 to 1967.

10. This PEI community was known to natives as *Munuskooch*.

QUIZ # 77

1. Which Newfoundland author wrote the novel *Random Passage*?

2. He was the last Conservative premier of Nova Scotia before Robert Stanfield.

3. What is the largest bay in the Gulf of St. Lawrence?

4. This Halifax-born member of The Mamas & The Papas died January 19, 2007.

5. Which Newfoundland community is the home of Sir Wilfred Grenfell College?

6. This Carly Simon song mentions Nova Scotia.

7. This New Brunswick engineer invented the variable-pitch airplane propeller.

8. This PEI author's book *The Alpine Path: The Story of My Career* was originally published in 1917.

9. He served as lieutenant-governor of Newfoundland from 1957 to 1963.

10. In 1994, this filmmaker's *Speak It! From the Heart of Black Nova Scotia* won a Gemini Award.

QUIZ # 78

1. In 2003, this co-founder of the *Amethyst Review* published the collection of poetry *Clarity That Is Darkness*.

2. This experimental solar building was constructed at Spry Point, PEI, in 1976.

3. What four colours are represented in the official flag of Newfoundland and Labrador?

4. The community of New Minas, Nova Scotia, sits on the bank of which river?

5. This British army officer, who led the British retreat from Concord, helped create the province of New Brunswick.

6. Bathurst, New Brunswick, is located in this county.

7. Mockbeggar is part of which Newfoundland community?

8. Stanley Redman's 1981 book, *Open Gangway*, deals with 1945 riots in this Nova Scotia city.

9. This noted naturalist did some of his paintings of birds while staying at Government House in Fredericton.

10. Mary Stuart Sage's 1973 book features the story of settlers brought to Belfast, PEI, by this Scottish aristocrat.

QUIZ # 79

1. The community of Norris Arm is near the mouth of which Newfoundland river?

2. This Nova Scotia author's 1976 autobiography is called *In My Time*.

3. This New Brunswick county calls itself "The Covered Bridge Capital of Atlantic Canada."

4. In 2006, this owner of Sandbar Music received a Music PEI award.

5. This French explorer set sail for Newfoundland on May 19, 1535.

6. *Stories of a River*, by Lloyd Hatcher Balah, is a collection of stories about this Nova Scotia river.

7. Which New Brunswick author wrote *The Elephant Talks to God*?

8. Toronto is in which PEI county?

9. Which singer/songwriter from Newfoundland wrote the song "Welcome To My Island, Mister Jones"?

10. Kemptville is in which Nova Scotia county?

QUIZ # 80

1. What is the largest university in the Maritimes?

2. This is the province with the highest population density in Canada.

3. Which Newfoundland union leader founded the *Fishermen's Advocate*?

4. This author won the 2003 Thomas Head Raddall Atlantic Fiction Award for her book *Downhill Chance*.

5. Gagetown is in which New Brunswick county?

6. This lawyer, politician, and judge served as lieutenant-governor of PEI from 1874 to 1879.

7. This community in Notre Dame Bay, Newfoundland, was once called Ship Cove.

8. Kay Hill's book about this man is subtitled *The Man Who Was Nova Scotia*.

9. This New Brunswick craftsman was known as "the one who made wood pray."

10. The village of Wellington is in which PEI county?

QUIZ # 81

1. Newfoundland's first Court of the Admiralty was held in this community in 1615.

2. This resident of Nova Scotia is the author of the *Martin Bridge* series of children's books.

3. This fort near Sackville, New Brunswick, became a national historic park in 1926.

4. Which golf course is located in Brudenell River, PEI?

5. Who was the first Church of England clergyman in Newfoundland?

6. This Nova Scotia community was once called Port Roseway.

7. This New Brunswick-born jockey rode Secretariat to the Triple Crown in 1973.

8. This Nova Scotia schooner with a Newfoundland crew ran contraband to PEI during the Prohibition years.

9. What do Newfoundlanders call thin strips of wood used as kindling?

10. This controversial fiddler from Nova Scotia released the album *Helter's Celtic* in 1999.

QUIZ # 82

1. This New Brunswick company produced Canada's first lollipops.

2. This is the official tree of PEI.

3. This Newfoundland premier sometimes called himself "the only living Father of Confederation."

4. The community of Laconia is in which Nova Scotia county?

5. Who succeeded Walter E. Foster as premier of New Brunswick?

6. This unincorporated area on PEI was originally called Connaught.

7. A 1929 tidal wave on the south coast of this Newfoundland peninsula claimed twenty-seven lives.

8. This Cape Breton trail is named after a famous European explorer.

9. The New Brunswick community of Petit Rocher is in which bay?

10. What is the easternmost point of mainland Canada?

QUIZ # 83

1. Paul O'Neill's history of this Newfoundland port is called *The Oldest City*.

2. Canso, Nova Scotia, is on the shore of which bay?

3. This famous hotel first opened in St. Andrews, New Brunswick, in June 1889.

4. The town of Stratford is in which PEI county?

5. In Newfoundland, the term "fish" traditionally referred to which species?

6. This curler from Charlottetown, PEI, played second on the team that won the 2001 World Junior Curling Championships.

7. The name of this New Brunswick town comes from the Mi'kmaq for "ideal camping ground."

8. She illustrated such books as *Lobster in My Pocket* and *Bud the Spud*.

9. Western Brook Pond is in which Newfoundland park?

10. This man, who fiddled regularly on the BBC during World War II, was born at Judique, Nova Scotia, in 1911.

QUIZ # 84

1. In which New Brunswick community could you visit the Ross Memorial Museum?

2. This premier of PEI served four terms as mayor of Summerside.

3. He wrote the hymn "We Love the Place, O God" while a clergyman at Trinity, Trinity Bay, Newfoundland.

4. The community of Londonderry is in which Nova Scotia county?

5. The name of this New Brunswick community comes from the Maliseet for "straight stream."

6. This Acadian lieutenant-governor of PEI was born at North Rustico on June 10, 1922.

7. Which strait separates the Labrador Sea from Baffin Bay?

8. *Lures*, a novel by this author residing in Nova Scotia, was nominated for the 2003 Thomas Head Raddall Atlantic Fiction Award.

9. The community of Riverview, New Brunswick, is near which city?

10. He was appointed PEI's poet laureate in 2004.

QUIZ # 85

1. This MP from St. John's East became Canada's minister of fisheries and oceans in 1979.

2. This Nova Scotian's book, *Memoirs of a Lightkeeper's Son*, was published in 2003.

3. This New Brunswick poet was the first English Canadian to publish a book-length poem.

4. The name of this PEI community was changed from Barrett's Cross in 1862.

5. The Viking Trail is on which Newfoundland peninsula?

6. Allister MacGillivray's 1981 book, *The Cape Breton Fiddler*, features this musician.

7. What is the official tree of New Brunswick?

8. This man from Three Rivers served as lieutenant-governor of PEI from 1884 to 1889.

9. In 1842, this geologist published *Excursions in and about Newfoundland During the Years 1839 and 1840*.

10. Loch Broom is in which Nova Scotia county?

QUIZ # 86

1. This New Brunswick politician served as minister of customs and minister of finance under John A. Macdonald.

2. She was known as the poet laureate of the Mi'kmaq and received the Order of Canada in 1989.

3. What is the name given to the sealing area northeast of Newfoundland?

4. Mark Finnan's 1997 book, *The First Nova Scotian*, deals with this short-lived early Nova Scotia settlement.

5. Newcastle is in which New Brunswick county?

6. What is the English translation of Bras d'Or?

7. This Dutch admiral captured St. John's, Newfoundland, on June 6, 1665.

8. In 2003, this founding member of April Wine was awarded the ECMA Lifetime Achievement Award.

9. This man served as premier of New Brunswick from 1883 to 1896.

10. This PEI locality was once called Princetown.

QUIZ # 87

1. This island community is fifteen kilometres south of Burgeo, Newfoundland.

2. This college in Cape Breton was founded by A. W. R. MacKenzie to preserve the Gaelic language, arts, and culture.

3. This New Brunswick island has been called "Canada's Emerald Isle."

4. This son of a former premier became premier of PEI on June 12, 2007.

5. These British aviators took off from Newfoundland in 1919 and made the first non-stop flight across the Atlantic.

6. In 1973, this well-known author published *Nova Scotia: Window on the Sea*.

7. This New Brunswick community claims to have the only harness shop in North America that produces handmade horse collars.

8. Who was the second colonial governor of PEI?

9. This female author from Newfoundland wrote *Cold Pastoral* and *The Eyes of the Gull*.

10. Bridgetown, Nova Scotia, is near which river?

QUIZ # 88

1. The community of Dark Harbour is on which New Brunswick island?

2. This Presbyterian minister from PEI ran for the leadership of the Manitoba Liberal party three times.

3. What do Newfoundlanders call a patch of open water surrounded by ice?

4. This community in Antigonish County, Nova Scotia, was once called Manchester Road.

5. What is the only constitutionally bilingual province in Canada?

6. Millbrook First Nation is located in which province?

7. Who succeeded James McGrath as lieutenant-governor of Newfoundland?

8. This is Nova Scotia's official gemstone.

9. This French daily newspaper, published in Moncton, New Brunswick, folded in 1988.

10. Portage became part of this PEI community in 1983.

QUIZ # 89

1. In 1966, this well-known Newfoundland broadcaster published *The Troubled Air*.

2. This community in Antigonish County, Nova Scotia, was once called Pomquette Forks.

3. This New Brunswick captain established the first settlement on Campobello Island.

4. Lucille H. Campey's 2001 book, *A Very Fine Class of Immigrants*, deals with settlers who came from this part of the United Kingdom.

5. Which Newfoundland community was home to the Lucky Strike mine?

6. In 2000, this author from Nova Scotia published the award-winning *Purple for Sky*.

7. The Ganong chocolate empire began in this New Brunswick community.

8. She is known as the last member of the Beothuk.

9. This Labrador community was once called Kauk Harbour.

10. In 1982, this singer from Nova Scotia released the album *The Hottest Night of the Year*.

QUIZ # 90

1. This New Brunswick city's Loyalist Days commemorate the landing of United Empire Loyalists here in 1783.

2. A famous UFO sighting took place in this Nova Scotia community in October 1967.

3. This Newfoundland-born actress portrayed Mary Mercer in *Of the Fields, Lately*.

4. This Nova Scotia lake and the surrounding area were known to natives as *Kespoogwit*, which means "land's end."

5. Who became premier of New Brunswick immediately after Raymond Frenette?

6. Sherwood became part of this PEI municipality in 1995.

7. This Newfoundland race claims to be North America's oldest continuous sporting event.

8. Who was the second premier of the colony of Nova Scotia?

9. Which New Brunswick community was originally called Gretna Green?

10. In 1980, this hockey player from PEI won the NHL's Bill Masterton Memorial Trophy.

QUIZ # 91

1. This Newfoundlander's recording of "The Alphabet Song" was a Canadian bestseller in 1972.

2. This Nova Scotia community was originally called Upper Chebogue.

3. In which New Brunswick community can you visit the Restigouche Gallery?

4. In 1982, this man from PEI became Canada's minister of justice.

5. Which Newfoundland cape is the most easterly point of land in North America?

6. This hockey player from Truro, Nova Scotia, is credited with helping erase professional hockey's "colour barrier."

7. This New Brunswick author won the Canada–Australia Literary Prize for his work, including *For Those Who Hunt the Wounded Down*.

8. This PEI community was once called Trois Rivières.

9. This Newfoundland author collaborated with Harold Horwood to write *Death on the Ice*.

10. From 1784 to 1820, this city was the capital of the British colony of Cape Breton Island.

QUIZ # 92

1. Which New Brunswick community is home to the Maritime College of Forest Technology?

2. This hockey player from PEI coached the Colorado Rockies and the New Jersey Devils.

3. What is the official bird of Newfoundland and Labrador?

4. The community of Mayflower is in which Nova Scotia county?

5. Samuel de Champlain sailed into the harbour of Saint John on this date, also known as the feast day of St. John the Baptist.

6. Natives called this PEI bay *Peetcook*.

7. This anti-Confederation soldier and politician was born at Cape Broyle, Newfoundland, on March 8, 1890.

8. *Únamakika* is the Mi'kmaq name for this island in Nova Scotia.

9. New Brunswick borders which American state?

10. In 2006, this dancer and fiddler created her own show, *Celtic Blaze*, as part of the Charlottetown Festival.

QUIZ # 93

1. The Newfoundland community of Lamaline is on which peninsula?

2. Fairfax Downey's 1965 book, subtitled *Key to a Continent*, features this early Nova Scotia settlement.

3. This co-founder of MGM studios grew up in Saint John, New Brunswick.

4. This PEI bay was once called Harris Bay.

5. His compilation *The Old Time Songs and Poetry of Newfoundland* was first published in 1927.

6. Earlier names for this community in Antigonish County, Nova Scotia, were Black River and Beauly.

7. This "Father of Biblical Studies in Canada" was born at Chatham, New Brunswick, in 1847.

8. This is the highest point in New Brunswick.

9. The entrance to the harbour of St. John's, Newfoundland, is known by what name?

10. Merigomish is in which Nova Scotia county?

QUIZ # 94

1. In which New Brunswick community could you visit *Le Village Historique Acadien*?

2. Miawpukek First Nation is located in this province.

3. This Memorial University of Newfoundland professor earned renown for his study of giant squid.

4. William Charles McKinnon's novel *The Midnight Murder* is based on an 1833 murder and triple hanging in this Nova Scotia port.

5. This orator became premier of New Brunswick in 1911.

6. Point Aconi sits at the northeastern tip of this Nova Scotia island.

7. Who succeeded Roger Grimes as premier of Newfoundland and Labrador?

8. This Gaelic name for Alexander Graham Bell's summer home at Baddeck, Nova Scotia, means "beautiful mountain."

9. The New Brunswick town of Woodstock is in which county?

10. This province has a roughly crescent shape.

QUIZ # 95

1. What is Canada's most easterly national park?

2. *Beyond the Atlantic Roar*, a 1974 book by Donald Campbell and R. A. MacLean, is a study of this immigrant group.

3. In which New Brunswick community can you view the Reversing Falls?

4. This famous Mi'kmaq activist from Nova Scotia involved in the American Indian Movement was murdered in 1976.

5. This Newfoundland community was originally called Little Placentia.

6. This author won the 2001 Dublin Literary Award for *No Great Mischief*.

7. Which animal is featured on the flag of New Brunswick?

8. This community in Cardigan Bay is considered PEI's only deepwater port.

9. The book *The Beothucks, or Red Indians*, by this Newfoundlander, was first published in 1915.

10. Jonathan McCully was one of four Fathers of Confederation born in this Nova Scotia community.

QUIZ # 96

1. In which New Brunswick community could you visit Richibucto River Museum?

2. Who succeeded Tom Rideout as premier of Newfoundland and Labrador?

3. In 1997, this historian from Nova Scotia published *John Cabot & the Voyage of the Matthew*.

4. This artist's sculpture at Escuminac, New Brunswick, marks the deaths of thirty-five fishermen in a 1959 storm.

5. Stanhope became part of this PEI community in 1974.

6. What was the original name given to permanent residents of Newfoundland?

7. Cape Breton Island is divided into how many counties?

8. This man from New Brunswick is believed to be Canada's first horticulturist.

9. In 1977, this poet from PEI published *Jackpine Sonnets*.

10. In the 1970s this archaeologist uncovered documents identifying the Basque whaling station at Red Bay, Labrador.

QUIZ # 97

1. This is the official mineral of Nova Scotia.

2. The name of this New Brunswick community is believed to have come from the Mi'kmaq for "river of many cliffs."

3. This foot-pounding folk icon born in New Brunswick and raised in PEI wrote and sang "The Hockey Song."

4. This co-discoverer of insulin died in a plane crash near Musgrave Harbour, Newfoundland, in 1941.

5. These two Atlantic Canadian provinces joined Confederation in 1867.

6. This New Brunswick community was formerly called Anderson Siding.

7. Ed Ives' 1971 book about this man is subtitled *The Farmer Poet of Prince Edward Island*.

8. This man, born in Campbellton, Newfoundland, became Canada's chief of defence staff in February 2005.

9. In 1928, this author from Nova Scotia published *Wooden Ships and Iron Men*.

10. This New Brunswick publication was the first penny newspaper in the British Empire.

QUIZ # 98

1. This comedian from PEI directed *Wiener Takes All*, a documentary about dachshund racing.

2. He founded the community of Trepassey, Newfoundland, in 1618.

3. This renowned fiddler was born at Margaree Forks, Nova Scotia, in 1908.

4. The New Brunswick community of Sussex is in which valley?

5. Lennox Island First Nation is located in this province.

6. In 1704 this captain fought off a French attack on the Newfoundland port of Bonavista.

7. In 1997, this former chief of Nova Scotia's Chapel Island First Nation released the poetry collection *Clay Pots and Bones*.

8. She was the first female mayor of Saint John.

9. Rosebank became part of which PEI community in 1995?

10. What was the first name of Viking explorer Karlsefni, who came to Newfoundland and Labrador around 1000 AD?

QUIZ # 99

1. This is Canada's second smallest province.

2. This New Brunswick military town is situated near the confluence of the Saint John and Jemseg rivers.

3. In 2004, this Newfoundland filmmaker produced the award-winning film *Pleasant Street*.

4. Marble Mountain is near which Newfoundland city?

5. In 1995, this singing family from Nova Scotia released the album *Grey Dusk of Eve*.

6. This was declared New Brunswick's official bird on August 13, 1983.

7. This fiddler from Antigonish County, Nova Scotia, was nicknamed "The Polka King."

8. "Seek ye first the kingdom of God" is the motto of this province.

9. This community in Victoria County, Nova Scotia, was once called Young's Cove.

10. This well-known artist and professor designed the Moncton 100 Monument.

QUIZ # 100

1. From 1998 to 2000, this actress from PEI played the title character in *Emily of New Moon*.

2. What is the name for a harp seal just past the whitecoat stage?

3. This river in Nova Scotia was named after Cap de la Hève, France, by Sieur de Monts in 1604.

4. Kouchibouguac National Park is in which New Brunswick county?

5. His *History of Prince Edward Island* was published in 1875 and reprinted in 1972.

6. Tradition holds that John Cabot landed at Cape Bonavista, Newfoundland, in what year?

7. This Nova Scotia river was known to early French settlers as Rivière des Habitants.

8. Which New Brunswick author wrote *Both Sides of the Wire*?

9. Elsipogtog First Nation is located in this province.

10. The Newfoundland community of Carbonear is in which bay?

Answers

QUIZ # 1

1. iceberg
2. Marion Robertson
3. Ted Williams
4. Park Corner
5. William Epps Cormack
6. Springhill
7. Bathurst
8. Allan Rankin
9. Cape Chidley
10. Spanish Bay

QUIZ # 2

1. Jacquet River
2. Milton Acorn
3. Humber River
4. Colleen Jones
5. Moncton
6. Annandale
7. "I'se the Bye"
8. Acadia University
9. Saint John
10. Teresa Doyle

QUIZ # 3

1. John Whitney Pickersgill
2. Joyce Barkhouse
3. Thomas Carleton
4. Montague
5. Cathy Jones
6. Windsor
7. Fundy National Park
8. *The Daily News*
9. Robert Hayman
10. Enos Collins

QUIZ # 4

1. James F. McCurdy
2. Georgetown
3. Earl Pilgrim
4. The Cottars
5. William George Richardson Hind
6. Harmony
7. Treaty of Paris
8. Sidney Crosby
9. Harrison and Wallace McCain
10. Borden

QUIZ # 5

1. Benevolent Irish Society
2. Nancy Garapick
3. Charlotte County
4. Harry Baglole
5. Carbonear
6. Rodney MacDonald
7. Julia Beckwith
8. Albion
9. switchel
10. Harry Bruce

QUIZ # 6

1. Francis Peabody Sharp
2. Derby
3. Placentia
4. 1749
5. K. C. Irving
6. Janet McGarry
7. Elliston
8. Gordon S. Harrington
9. Mactaquac
10. Hillsborough (East) River

QUIZ # 7

1. Brad Gushue
2. 1855
3. *l'Evangeline*
4. Belfast
5. St. John's
6. Rose Fortune
7. Robert Foulis
8. Dundas
9. Amelia Earhart
10. James Boyle Uniacke

QUIZ # 8

1. Bouctouche
2. St. John's
3. copper
4. George Elliott Clarke
5. Charles Connell
6. Malpeque Bay
7. Samuel Codner
8. Acadia
9. Alden Nowlan
10. Iris

QUIZ # 9

1. Joao Alvares Fagundes
2. Dartmouth
3. Frank McKenna
4. Michael Hennessey
5. Sir Francis Pickmore
6. Sandra and Ron Lightburn
7. Grace Lockhart
8. Hunter River
9. Port aux Basques
10. Halifax

QUIZ # 10

1. Fredericton
2. Selkirk
3. Arthur Scammell
4. Glooscap
5. Maisonnette
6. Avalon
7. Sir Humphrey Gilbert
8. Russell MacLellan
9. Saint John County
10. Churchill

QUIZ #11

1. rug-hooking
2. Men of the Deeps
3. Rosemarie Landry
4. Aubin E. Arsenault
5. Aguathuna
6. Canso Causeway
7. Gagetown
8. Boston
9. Harry Brown
10. Bay of Fundy

QUIZ #12

1. Acadians
2. Cornwall
3. Hazel Newhook and Lynn Verge
4. J. P. Cormier
5. Jean Baptiste Louis Franquelin
6. Avondale
7. seal hunt
8. Robert L. Stanfield
9. Shawn Graham
10. Wayne Johnston

Answers

QUIZ #13

1. Hibernia
2. Sheldon Currie
3. Alex Colville
4. Keith Milligan
5. Newfoundland and Labrador
6. John Hamm
7. George King
8. Dunk River
9. Brian Tobin
10. Ecum Secum

QUIZ #14

1. Clair
2. A. Murray MacKay Bridge
3. Grand Lake
4. Sam Moon
5. Nepisiguit River
6. Jerome
7. Marystown
8. Richard Uniacke
9. Jonathan Odell
10. Lady Slipper

QUIZ #15

1. Francisco de Pinedo
2. J. F. W. DesBarres
3. George F. Matthew
4. Elmira
5. William Gosling
6. Ellen Page
7. Grand Manan Island
8. Joel Hynes
9. John Bingley Garland
10. April Wine

QUIZ #16

1. Ivan "Bill" Crowell
2. Les Araynes
3. St. Pierre and Miquelon
4. Alfred Silver
5. St. John River
6. Dr. John Smith
7. *The Vikings*
8. Mulgrave
9. Shepody Bay
10. Cabot Tower

Answers

QUIZ #17

1. Leonidas Hubbard
2. Antigonish
3. Andrew Wetmore
4. Joseph H. Sherman
5. Marysvale
6. Benjamin Moir
7. Florenceville
8. NSCAD University
9. Joseph "Joey" Smallwood
10. Pugwash

QUIZ #18

1. Raymond Frenette
2. Grace Butt
3. Bridgewater
4. Joseph M. Augustine
5. River Clyde
6. Entente Cordiale
7. Bruce Armstrong
8. Bricklin
9. Patricia Murray
10. Mary Lou Farrell

QUIZ #19

1. Northumberland Strait
2. David Adams Richards
3. Pat Binns
4. Fort Pepperell
5. *The Vanishing Cape Breton Fiddler*
6. Restigouche River
7. Art Gallery of Nova Scotia
8. Ernest Howse
9. Antigonish County
10. Charles Richards

QUIZ #20

1. Stanley Bridge
2. Elizabeth Goudie
3. Sydney
4. William B. Jack
5. Stratford
6. Strait of Belle Isle
7. C. D. Howe
8. Victoria County
9. Doug MacLean
10. E. J. Pratt

Answers

QUIZ #21

1. Grosses Coques
2. Quebec
3. Great Big Sea
4. Deer Lake
5. Ruby Keeler
6. 1984
7. Kingston
8. Buddy Wasisname and the Other Fellers
9. Amherst
10. St. Andrews

QUIZ # 22

1. Annapolis Royal
2. John Clinch
3. Daniel M. "Dan" Petrie
4. Yvon Durelle
5. Walter M. Lea
6. Splinter Fleet
7. piping plover
8. Middle Island
9. Prince County
10. Albert B. Perlin

QUIZ # 23

1. Daniel N. Paul
2. Mount Allison University
3. 1534
4. Long Point Lighthouse
5. Rans Bucknam (Bucknam Pasha)
6. J. J. Fraser
7. Summerside
8. unicorn
9. Melanie Doane
10. Shediac

QUIZ # 24

1. Tusket River
2. Tom Cahill
3. Chester
4. Winnifred Blair
5. Hiram Blanchard
6. Terra Nova National Park
7. John Allan Cameron
8. St. Leonard
9. Moosehead
10. John Crosbie

Answers

QUIZ # 25

1. Judique
2. New Brunswick
3. *Bluenose*
4. L'Anse-aux-Meadows
5. Portia White
6. Passamaquoddy Bay
7. "a pleasant piece of land"
8. Michael F. Harrington
9. *Silver Dart*
10. Moncton

QUIZ # 26

1. Neil McLeod
2. Baie Verte
3. Admiral Peter Warren
4. Sir Charles G. D. Roberts
5. Prince County
6. *All Around the Circle*
7. Chebogue
8. Bristol
9. PEI
10. Captain Bob Bartlett

QUIZ # 27

1. Kentville
2. Captain George Anderson
3. Caledonia
4. longers
5. Crescent Beach
6. New Brunswick
7. Helena Squires
8. Cyril MacPhee
9. J. W. Giles
10. Belfast

QUIZ # 28

1. Johnny Burke
2. David Manners
3. Nepisiguit River
4. Jodie Samuelson
5. White Bay
6. St. Francis Xavier University
7. Earl of Orkney
8. McCain
9. George Decker
10. Cumberland Basin

Answers

QUIZ # 29

1. Bernard Lord
2. Bedeque Bay and Malpeque Bay
3. Baccalieu
4. eleven
5. Restigouche County
6. Hamilton
7. Wilfred Grenfell
8. John Brophy
9. Miramichi Bay
10. Labrador Straits Museum

QUIZ # 30

1. Fabian O'Dea
2. Mersey River
3. H. J. Flemming
4. Sarah McLachlan
5. Great Northern Peninsula
6. India Pale Ale
7. Fredericton
8. Lori Kane
9. Placentia
10. John Gracie

QUIZ #31

1. Université de Moncton
2. Brudenell River
3. Herbert Pottle
4. Richmond County
5. Bathurst
6. Jedediah S. Carvell
7. a wave on the water
8. Lennie Gallant
9. New England
10. Mike Duffy

QUIZ # 32

1. Knights of Columbus Hostel
2. *Street Cents*
3. Harlan C. Brewster
4. Bob MacMillan
5. James Cook
6. Carole MacNeil
7. York County
8. Souris
9. Labrador Current
10. Sir Charles Tupper

Answers

QUIZ # 33

1. Benedict Arnold
2. Rustico
3. Joseph "Joey" Smallwood
4. Dufferin
5. Shediac
6. Robert A. Falconer
7. Cape Bonavista
8. Gerald Regan
9. Dieppe
10. seven

QUIZ # 34

1. Rufus Guinchard
2. *Evangeline*
3. A. E. Ritchie
4. Summerside
5. Whale's Gulch
6. Moosehead
7. Miramichi River
8. Robert Campbell
9. Duckworth Street
10. Lynn Davies

QUIZ # 35

1. Labrador
2. Queens County
3. Levi Chafe
4. Alexa McDonough
5. Oromocto
6. Brenton Harold "Jack" Turner
7. Frederick C. Alderdice
8. Quoddy Harbour
9. John Thompson
10. Donald Sutherland

QUIZ # 36

1. Lewisporte
2. Cunard
3. H. J. Flemming
4. Morell River
5. Sir William Coaker
6. Moses Michael Coady
7. Fredericton
8. Atlantic Film Festival
9. Placentia Bay
10. Afton River

Answers

QUIZ # 37

1. Mount Allison University
2. Richard Terfry
3. Anne Stine Ingstad
4. Dominion
5. Thomas Carleton
6. North Cape
7. Treaty of Versailles
8. 21
9. King's College
10. Terry Dunton Stevenson

QUIZ # 38

1. log driving
2. John S. Thompson
3. Dave Durepos
4. Egmont Bay
5. Signal Hill
6. Angus L. Macdonald Bridge
7. William Davidson
8. Central Kings
9. Richard Squires
10. Wedgeport

QUIZ # 39

1. Passamaquoddy Bay
2. blue, white, red, and gold
3. Catalina
4. Carol Ann Cole
5. Nakawic
6. Tara MacLean
7. Henry Mainwaring
8. Art Gallery of Newfoundland and Labrador
9. Caraquet
10. Harold, Steve, and Donnie Doyle

QUIZ # 40

1. ballycatter
2. Ephraim Atkinson
3. University of New Brunswick
4. Dunblane
5. Simani
6. Mabou
7. Massachusetts
8. Margie Carmichael
9. Quebec
10. Crystal Palace

Answers

QUIZ # 41

1. Florence Nightingale
2. PEI
3. Steve Neary
4. rug-hooking
5. Bartibog Bridge
6. Shubenacadie River
7. Castle Hill
8. Natalie MacMaster
9. Charles H. Doyle
10. Abells Cape

QUIZ # 42

1. killick
2. Cumberland Ship Railway
3. Pictou County
4. Randolph H. Nicholson
5. Bonne Bay
6. Reverend Norman McLeod
7. Walter Foster
8. Charlottetown
9. Rick Mercer
10. Sable Island

QUIZ # 43

1. Mount Carleton
2. Marion L. Reid
3. pitcher plant
4. Kidston Island
5. Charles de la Tour
6. Cascumpec Bay
7. David Buchan
8. Louisbourg
9. Christ Church
10. Prince County

QUIZ # 44

1. Bobbie Roberston
2. Linden MacIntyre
3. Madeleine A. Fritz
4. John H. Bell
5. Grand Bank
6. Alexander Keith
7. Restigouche County
8. St. John's
9. Georgina Stirling
10. Halifax

Answers

QUIZ # 45

1. Saint John
2. Joshua Slocum
3. Churchill River
4. *Saladin*
5. Moncton
6. Charles Andrew MacGillivray
7. Philip Francis Little
8. Greendale
9. *Spem reduxit*
10. PEI

QUIZ # 46

1. sled
2. Danny Gallivan
3. "Peter Emberley"
4. Kings County
5. Cavendish Boyle
6. Long Island
7. Fredericton
8. PEI
9. Sandwich Bay
10. New Scotland

QUIZ # 47

1. Alexander "Boss" Gibson
2. Cavendish Beach
3. Cross of St. George
4. Frankville
5. ten
6. Queens County
7. Sam LaFosse
8. Bras d'Or Lake
9. Robert Monckton
10. Joseph "Joey" Smallwood

QUIZ # 48

1. kayak
2. George Canyon
3. Tantramar
4. Rawlins Cross
5. George Allan England
6. Rita MacNeil
7. Dalton Camp
8. Kings County
9. Newfoundland
10. Hopewell

Answers

QUIZ # 49

1. Saint John
2. St. Peter's Bay
3. St. Anthony
4. James W. Johnston
5. Edmundston
6. Catherine Callbeck
7. Richard Brothers
8. Linda Johns
9. Robert "Robbie" Burns
10. Eastport Peninsula

QUIZ # 50

1. Stephen Kimber
2. Fredericton
3. Charlottetown
4. Roch Voisine
5. Hilda Woolnough
6. Charles Gorman
7. Mi'kmaq
8. cuddy
9. Sloan
10. Daniel d'Auger de Subercase

QUIZ # 51

1. Alberton
2. George Calvert
3. Steve Murphy
4. Kent County
5. St. Charles
6. 1960
7. Robert Aitken
8. Rogersville
9. PEI
10. Notre Dame Bay

QUIZ # 52

1. Sons of Maxwell
2. Richibucto River
3. Lesley Choyce
4. Algonquin
5. Colchester County
6. Muriel M. Fergusson
7. Bangor
8. Cape Spear
9. Dunvegan
10. Dr. James Keith Chapman

Answers

QUIZ # 53

1. Queens County
2. João Fernandes
3. Grand Pré
4. Moncton
5. Hurricane Juan
6. Gander River
7. Kejimkujik
8. Black's Harbour
9. Prince County
10. Joan Morrissey

QUIZ # 54

1. Stellarton
2. Hillsborough
3. Appalachian Mountains
4. Cupids
5. Allan "Al" MacInnis
6. Fredericton
7. October
8. Jack McDuff
9. Budge Wilson
10. Rita V. MacNeill

QUIZ # 55

1. Catherine MacLellan
2. snow flurry
3. Lewis MacKenzie
4. Old Sow
5. Bethel
6. Thomas Cochrane
7. Donna Morrissey
8. *Blue Water*
9. Prince County
10. Arctic tern

QUIZ # 56

1. Labradorian
2. Moncton
3. Ryan Anstey
4. William Anthony Paddon
5. Allister MacGillivray
6. Dorchester
7. Bedeque Bay
8. Ray Guy
9. Clydesdale
10. Emeric Essex Vidal

Answers

QUIZ # 57

1. Boughton Island
2. *Argyle*
3. Buddy MacMaster
4. St. Andrews
5. Mount Caubvick
6. Terre-Neuve-et-Labrador
7. Sharon Palermo
8. John Coffin
9. Kings County
10. *Florizel*

QUIZ # 58

1. Susan Kerslake
2. Machias Seal Island
3. Diane Nyland
4. whaling
5. New Brunswick
6. Franklin Delano Roosevelt
7. Summerside
8. dusk
9. Sissiboo River
10. *Marco Polo*

QUIZ # 59

1. Sloan
2. Dover
3. Austin Loomer Rand
4. Bliss Carman
5. Prince County
6. James F. Bancroft
7. Edith Comeau Tufts
8. Moncton Hawks
9. William Henry Pope
10. Thomas "Tommy" Ricketts

QUIZ # 60

1. Kings County
2. James H. Dunn
3. Mary Allison Doull
4. the *Sun*
5. Rita Joe
6. Webster–Ashburton Treaty
7. Souris
8. Harbour Grace
9. Nova Scotia
10. Chatham

Answers

QUIZ # 61

1. Hare Bay
2. Delmore W. (Buddy) Daye
3. Sir Charles G. D. Roberts
4. Kings County
5. Guglielmo Marconi
6. Anne Simpson
7. Gannet Rock
8. Milton Acorn
9. Joseph "Joey" Smallwood
10. *Mary Celeste*

QUIZ # 62

1. Walter Pidgeon
2. Prince County
3. Royal St. John's Regatta
4. Sarah McLachlan
5. Point Lepreau
6. Bob Stewart
7. Wabana
8. Ben Eoin
9. Joel Plaskett
10. Cardigan Bay

QUIZ # 63

1. David G. Pitt
2. John Savage
3. Shepody Bay
4. Cape Spear, Newfoundland
5. Union Jack
6. Parrsboro
7. Louis XV
8. Nouvelle-Écosse
9. *William Carson*
10. Kings County

QUIZ # 64

1. Doaktown
2. Jericho Road
3. Michael Crummey
4. Canning
5. Fredericton
6. Department of Veterans Affairs
7. Port au Choix
8. Don Aker
9. Nova Scotia
10. PE

Answers

QUIZ # 65

1. *Southern Cross*
2. Cumberland County
3. Lemuel John Tweedie
4. Miltonvale Park
5. Gordon Pinsent
6. Antigonish County
7. Alden Nowlan
8. Hillsborough Bay
9. Clarenville
10. Sydney

QUIZ # 66

1. Petit-Rocher
2. Lawrence Doyle
3. New World Island
4. Glen Murray
5. Edmundston
6. *Rockbound*
7. stationers
8. Holly Cole
9. Grand Manan Island
10. tidal bore

QUIZ # 67

1. Gaspar Corté Real
2. Newfoundland and Labrador
3. St. John River
4. Kings County
5. Richard Gwynn
6. Gaspereau
7. James Murchie
8. Rena McLean
9. Conception Bay
10. Nova Scotia

QUIZ # 68

1. Coverdale
2. Nancy White
3. Rex Murphy
4. Cape Breton County
5. "Main John" Glasier
6. Queens County
7. Great Auk
8. Bridgewater
9. Saint-Louis-de-Kent
10. Haywire

Answers

QUIZ # 69

1. Cape Ann or Sou'wester
2. Cole Harbour
3. poutines râpées
4. Hesketh Prichard
5. Ted Russell
6. Inverness County
7. James De Mille
8. Murray Harbour
9. HMS *Spitfire*
10. Annapolis Valley

QUIZ # 70

1. Shediac
2. Joe Ghiz
3. Labrador City
4. Jerry Byers
5. James "Bully" Forbes
6. Petitcodiac River
7. Peter Easton
8. White Juan
9. purple violet
10. Angèle Arsenault

QUIZ # 71

1. Joan Clark
2. Dunmaglass
3. Peter Mitchell
4. Queens County
5. puffin
6. *Cutty Sark*
7. Moncton
8. Ontario and Quebec
9. Ewart John Arlington Harnum
10. Chester

QUIZ # 72

1. bay of warmth
2. Chester
3. mouldy
4. Peter Donat
5. Drummond
6. St. Croix River
7. Johnny Dwyer
8. Cape George
9. Gilbert Finn
10. Stratford

Answers

QUIZ # 73

1. Portuguese White Fleet
2. Cape Breton Island
3. Fredericton
4. Paul Thompson
5. Baytona
6. Silas Tertius Rand
7. fiddlehead
8. Belfast
9. Wilfred Grenfell
10. Max Haines

QUIZ # 74

1. Tracadie
2. Basil King
3. "Newfie Bullet"
4. Bill Casey
5. Restigouche River
6. Richard Wood
7. John Kent
8. Mary Jane Lamond
9. John Gyles
10. Malpeque Bay

QUIZ # 75

1. *Christmas Seal*
2. St. Ann's, Nova Scotia
3. Miramichi River
4. Thomas McMillan
5. Mary Pratt
6. Digby County
7. Timothy W. Anglin
8. Souris
9. Robert Bond
10. Nova Scotia Agricultural College

QUIZ # 76

1. Hawks
2. David MacDonald
3. *Family Fireside*
4. Don Domanski
5. Partridge Island
6. Brad Richards
7. Notre Dame Bay
8. Antigonish County
9. Fred Cogswell
10. Miscouche

Answers

QUIZ # 77

1. Bernice Morgan
2. Gordon S. Harrington
3. Chaleur Bay
4. Denny Doherty
5. Corner Brook
6. "You're So Vain"
7. Wallace R. Turnbull
8. Lucy Maud Montgomery
9. Campbell MacPherson
10. Sylvia Hamilton

QUIZ # 78

1. Penny Ferguson
2. The Ark
3. white, blue, red, and gold
4. Cornwallis River
5. Edward Winslow
6. Gloucester County
7. Bonavista
8. Halifax
9. John James Audubon
10. Lord Selkirk

QUIZ # 79

1. Exploits River
2. Thomas H. Raddall
3. Kings County
4. Lloyd Doyle
5. Jacques Cartier
6. Margaree River
7. Dale Estey
8. Queens County
9. Roy Payne
10. Yarmouth County

QUIZ # 80

1. Dalhousie University
2. PEI
3. Sir William Coaker
4. Donna Morrissey
5. Queens County
6. Robert Hodgson
7. Botwood
8. Joseph Howe
9. Leon Leger
10. Prince County

Answers

QUIZ # 81

1. Trinity, Trinity Bay
2. Jessica Scott Kerrin
3. Fort Beausejour
4. Dundarave Golf Course
5. Erasmus Stourton
6. Shelburne
7. Ron Turcotte
8. *Nellie J. Banks*
9. splits
10. Ashley MacIsaac

QUIZ # 82

1. Ganong
2. red oak
3. Joseph "Joey" Smallwood
4. Lunenburg County
5. Peter John Veniot
6. New Harmony
7. Burin Peninsula
8. Cabot Trail
9. Nepisiguit Bay
10. Cape St. Charles, Labrador

QUIZ # 83

1. St. John's
2. Chedabucto Bay
3. Fairmont Algonquin
4. Queens County
5. codfish
6. Robyn MacPhee
7. Tracadie
8. Brenda Jones
9. Gros Morne National Park
10. Dan R. MacDonald

QUIZ # 84

1. St. Andrews
2. Albert Saunders
3. William J. Bullock
4. Colchester County
5. Nackawic
6. Joseph Aubin Doiron
7. Davis Strait
8. Susan Goyette
9. Moncton
10. Frank Ledwell

Answers

QUIZ # 85

1. James McGrath
2. Billy Budge
3. Oliver Goldsmith
4. Kensington
5. Great Northern Peninsula
6. Winston "Scotty" Fitzgerald
7. balsam fir
8. Andrew Archibald Macdonald
9. Joseph Beete Jukes
10. Pictou County

QUIZ # 86

1. Samuel Leonard Tilley
2. Rita Joe
3. The Front
4. Port Royal
5. Northumberland County
6. arms of gold
7. Michiel de Ruyter
8. Myles Goodwyn
9. Andrew George Blair
10. Malpeque

QUIZ # 87

1. Ramea
2. The Gaelic College of Celtic Arts and Crafts
3. Partridge Island
4. Robert Ghiz
5. John Alcock and Arthur Brown
6. Ernest Buckler
7. Sackville
8. Edmund Fanning
9. Margaret Duley
10. Annapolis River

QUIZ # 88

1. Grand Manan Island
2. Reverend Harold Lloyd Henderson
3. swatch
4. Marydale
5. New Brunswick
6. Nova Scotia
7. Frederick William Russell
8. agate
9. *Le Matin*
10. Lady Slipper

Answers

QUIZ # 89

1. Donald Jamieson
2. Heatherton
3. William Owen
4. Scotland
5. Buchans
6. Carol Bruneau
7. St. Stephen
8. Shanawdithit
9. Nain
10. Anne Murray

QUIZ # 90

1. Saint John
2. Shag Harbour
3. Flo Patterson
4. Lake Milo
5. Camille Theriault
6. Charlottetown
7. Royal St. John's Regatta
8. William Young
9. Douglastown
10. Al MacAdam

QUIZ # 91

1. Wilf Doyle
2. Arcadia
3. Campbellton
4. Mark MacGuigan
5. Cape Spear
6. Stan "Chook" Maxwell
7. David Adams Richards
8. Brudenell Point
9. Cassie Brown
10. Sydney

QUIZ # 92

1. Fredericton
2. William "Bill" MacMillan
3. puffin
4. Digby County
5. June 24, 1604
6. Bedeque Bay
7. Peter Cashin
8. Cape Breton Island
9. Maine
10. Stephanie Cadman

Answers

QUIZ # 93

1. Burin Peninsula
2. Louisbourg
3. Louis B. Mayer
4. Rustico Bay
5. Gerald S. Doyle
6. Glassburn
7. James Frederick McCurdy
8. Mount Carleton
9. The Narrows
10. Pictou County

QUIZ # 94

1. Caraquet
2. Newfoundland and Labrador
3. Frederick A. Aldrich
4. Sydney
5. James Kidd Flemming
6. Boularderie Island
7. Danny Williams
8. Beinn Bhreagh
9. Carleton County
10. PEI

QUIZ # 95

1. Terra Nova National Park
2. Scots
3. Saint John
4. Anna Mae Pictou Aquash
5. Argentia
6. Alistair MacLeod
7. lion
8. Georgetown
9. James Patrick Howley
10. Amherst

QUIZ # 96

1. Rexton
2. Clyde Wells
3. Brian Cuthbertson
4. Claude Roussel
5. North Shore
6. livyers
7. four
8. Francis Peabody Sharp
9. Milton Acorn
10. Selma Barkham

Answers

QUIZ # 97

1. stilbite
2. Sevogle
3. Stompin' Tom Connors
4. Dr. Frederick Banting
5. Nova Scotia and New Brunswick
6. Saint-Quentin
7. Lawrence Doyle
8. General Rick Hillier
9. Frederick William Wallace
10. *Saint John News*

QUIZ # 98

1. Shane MacDougall
2. William Vaughan
3. Angus Chisholm
4. Kennebecasis Valley
5. PEI
6. Captain Michael Gill
7. Lindsay Marshall
8. Elsie Wayne
9. Stratford
10. Thorfinn

QUIZ # 99

1. Nova Scotia
2. Gagetown
3. Gerry Rogers
4. Corner Brook
5. The Rankins
6. black-capped chickadee
7. Hugh Angus MacDonald
8. Newfoundland and Labrador
9. Dingwall
10. Claude Roussel

QUIZ # 100

1. Martha MacIsaac
2. beater
3. LaHave River
4. Kent County
5. Duncan Campbell
6. 1497
7. Cornwallis River
8. Ted Jones
9. New Brunswick
10. Conception Bay